THE CELL THEORY

Biology's Core Principle

BIOLOGY BOOK | SCIENCE GRADE 7 |
CHILDREN'S BIOLOGY BOOKS

First Edition, 2019

Published in the United States by Speedy Publishing LLC, 40 E Main Street, Newark, Delaware 19711 USA.

10 9 8 7 6 * 5 4 3 2 1

Print Edition: 9781541949539
Digital Edition: 9781541951334

See the world in pictures. Build your knowledge in style.
https://www.speedypublishing.com/

CONTENTS

In this book, we're going to talk about cell theory, the core principle of biology, so let's get right to it!

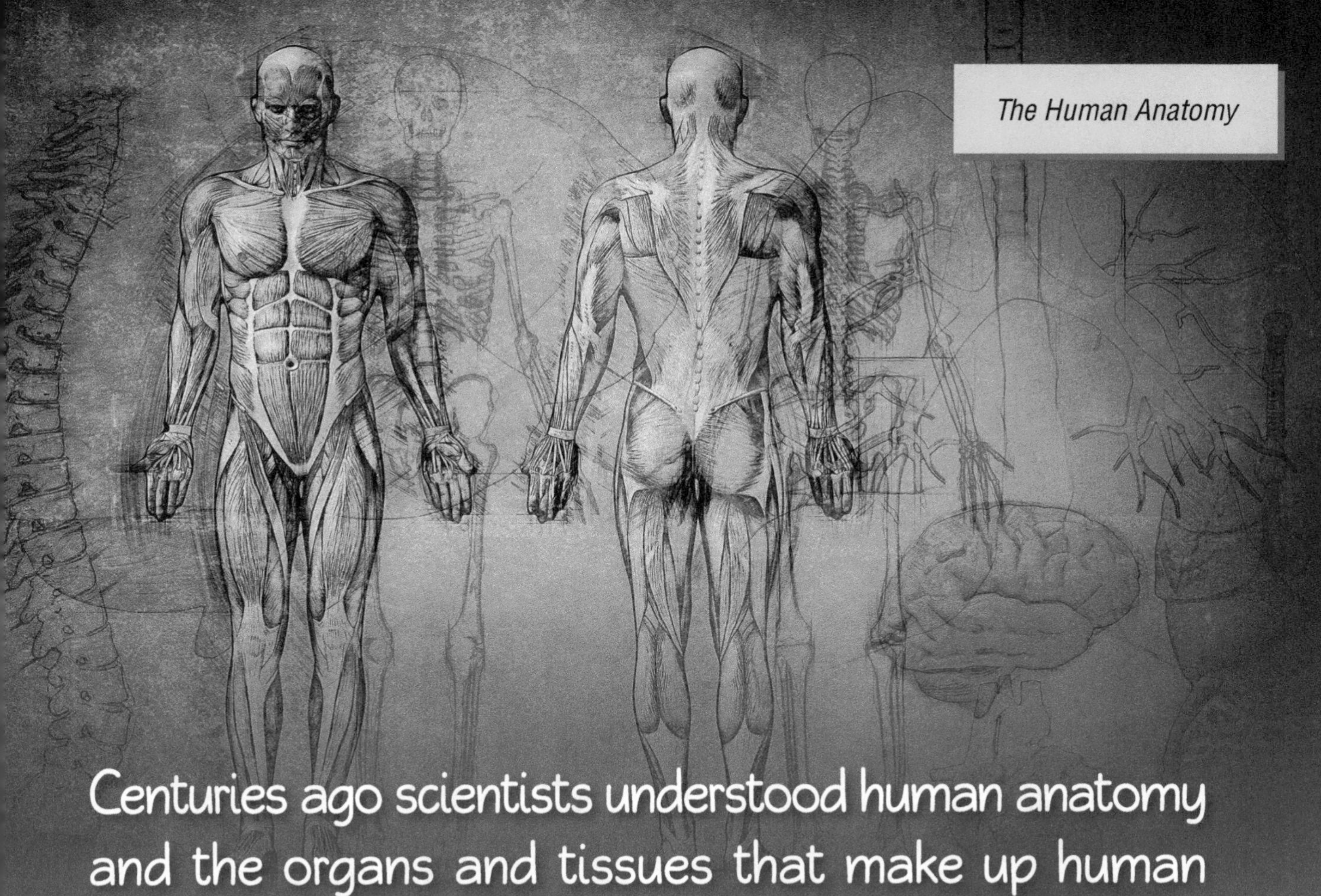

Centuries ago scientists understood human anatomy and the organs and tissues that make up human bodies. What they didn't know about was what they couldn't see. They couldn't tell what living tissue was made of, but that all began to change in 1665 when the scientist Robert Hooke invented the first light microscope.

A

ROBERT HOOKE INVENTS THE FIRST LIGHT MICROSCOPE

Robert Hooke

Hooke had a unique set of talents. He was a master at constructing instruments used for scientific study. He was also a very skilled artist. Hooke began making improvements to the compound microscope that biologists were using. One of his improvements was a new type of mechanism for focusing, which he had envisioned and designed.

Prior to this time, scientists had to move their specimens around to make sure they were in focus. The other crucial change he made was to add much better lighting so the specimens could be seen more clearly. He set up a small oil lamp next to the microscope. Then, he took a water lens and focused the light from the lamp onto the area of the microscope where specimens were placed for observation. With this better focus and bright lighting, specimens could be seen through the microscope many times better than they could have been seen before, which revealed many new details.

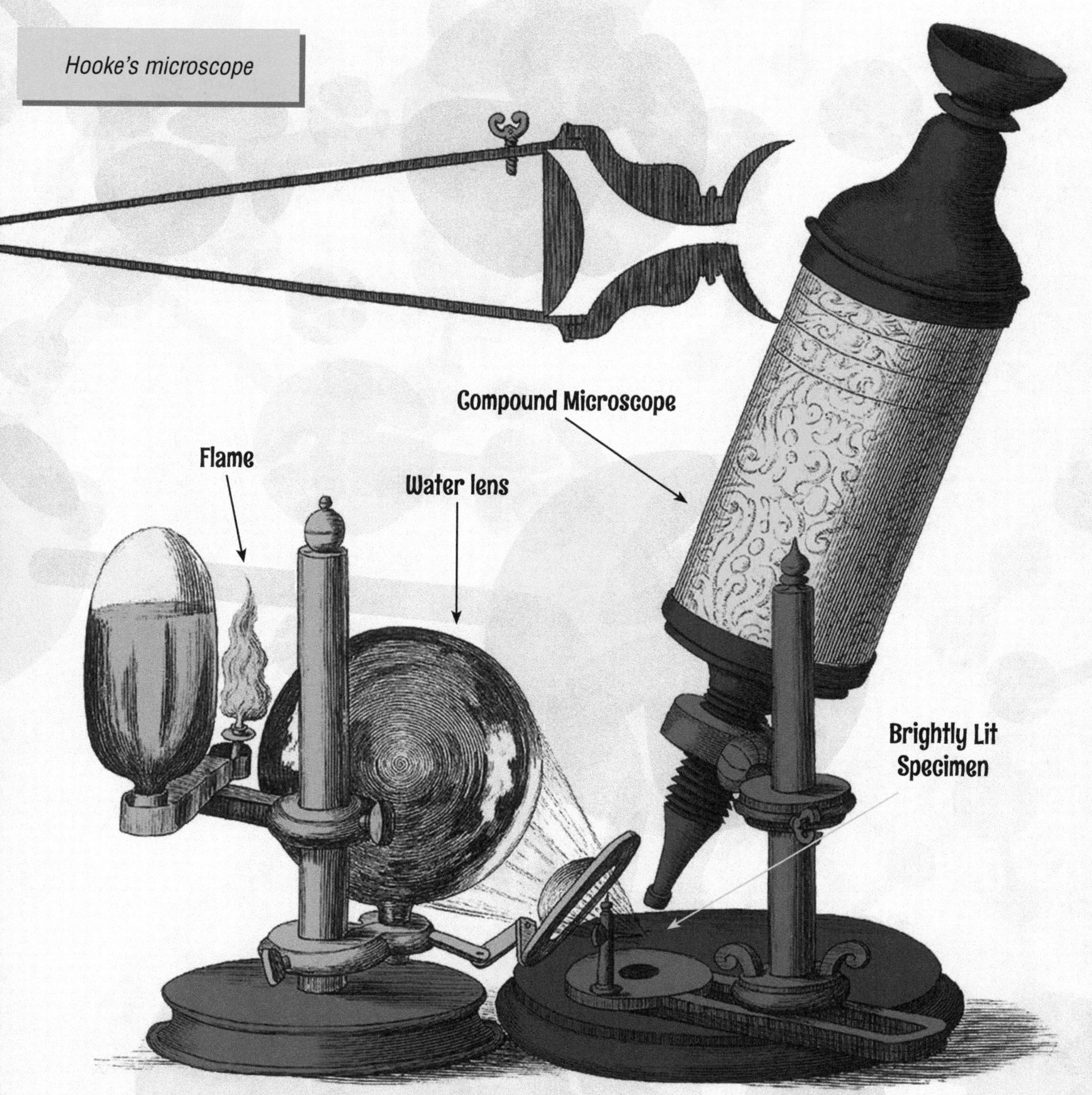
Hooke's microscope
Compound Microscope
Flame
Water lens
Brightly Lit
Specimen

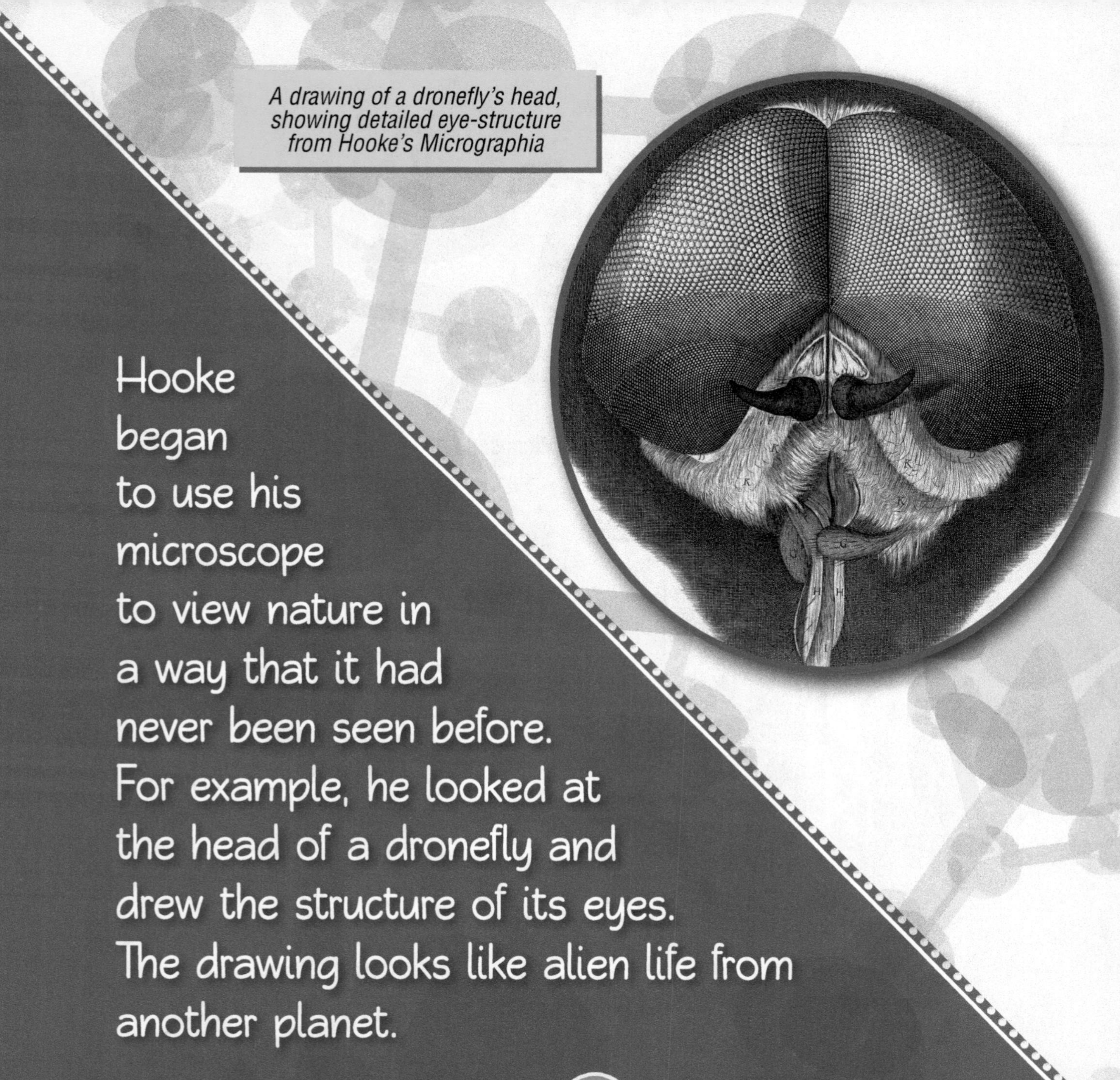

A drawing of a dronefly's head, showing detailed eye-structure from Hooke's Micrographia

Hooke began to use his microscope to view nature in a way that it had never been seen before. For example, he looked at the head of a dronefly and drew the structure of its eyes. The drawing looks like alien life from another planet.

Some people didn't believe the things that he had seen were real. Photography had not yet been invented so without Hooke's drawings, we would have no idea what he saw. He eventually published his findings in a book called Micrographia.

MICROGRAPHIA:
OR SOME
Physiological Descriptions
OF
MINUTE BODIES
MADE BY
MAGNIFYING GLASSES.
WITH
OBSERVATIONS and INQUIRIES thereupon.

By *R. HOOKE*, Fellow of the ROYAL SOCIETY.

Non possis oculo quantum contendere Linceus,
Non tamen idcirco contemnas Lippus inungi. Horat. Ep. lib. 1.

LONDON, Printed by *Jo. Martyn*, and *Ja. Allestry*, Printers to the ROYAL SOCIETY, and are to be sold at their Shop at the *Bell* in S. *Paul's* Church-yard. M DC LXV.

Title page of Hooke's book, "Micrographia"

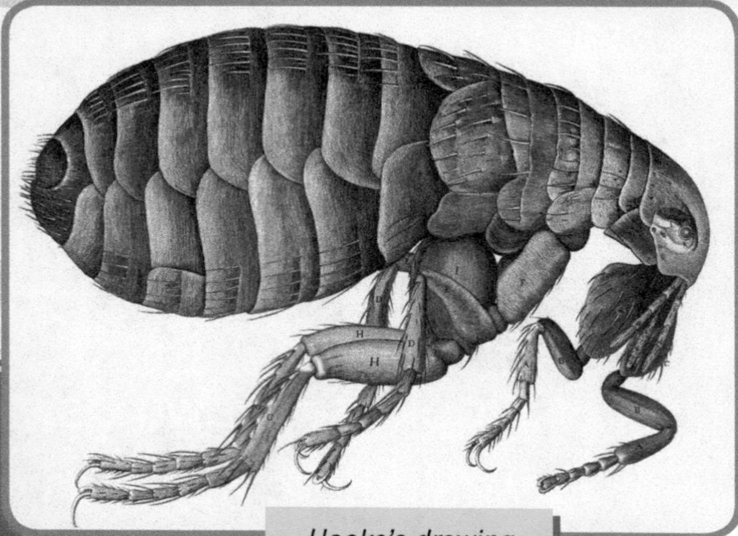

Hooke's drawing of a flea

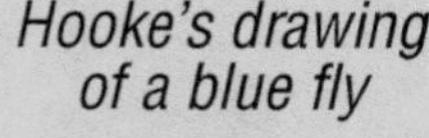

Hooke's drawing of a blue fly

His book became the first bestselling book in the field of science. People were fascinated and in some cases a little bit scared of his findings because they had never seen anything like it before.

Hooke's drawing of a louse

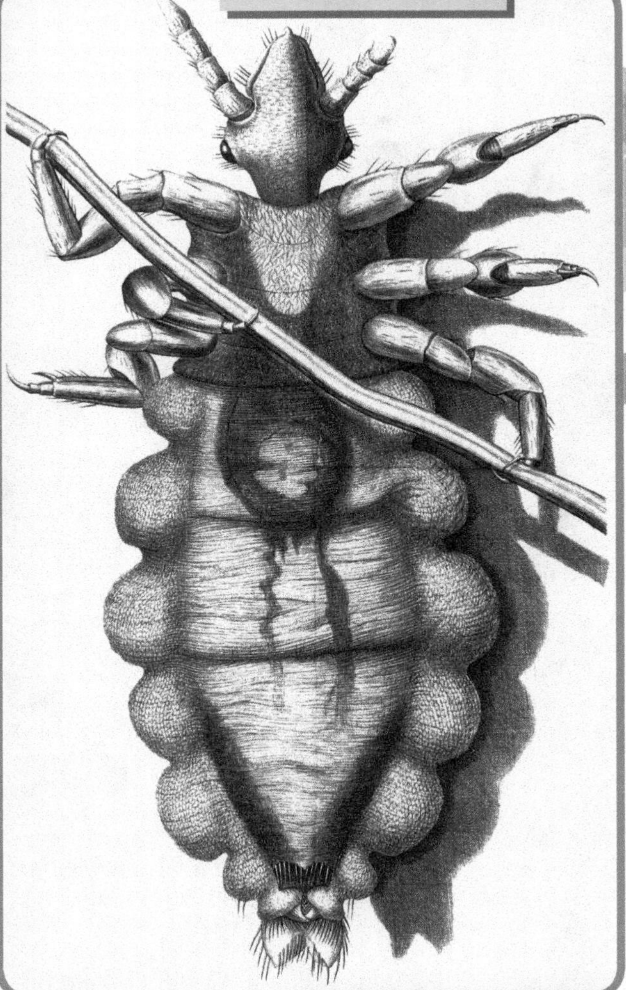

Hooke's drawing of a gnat

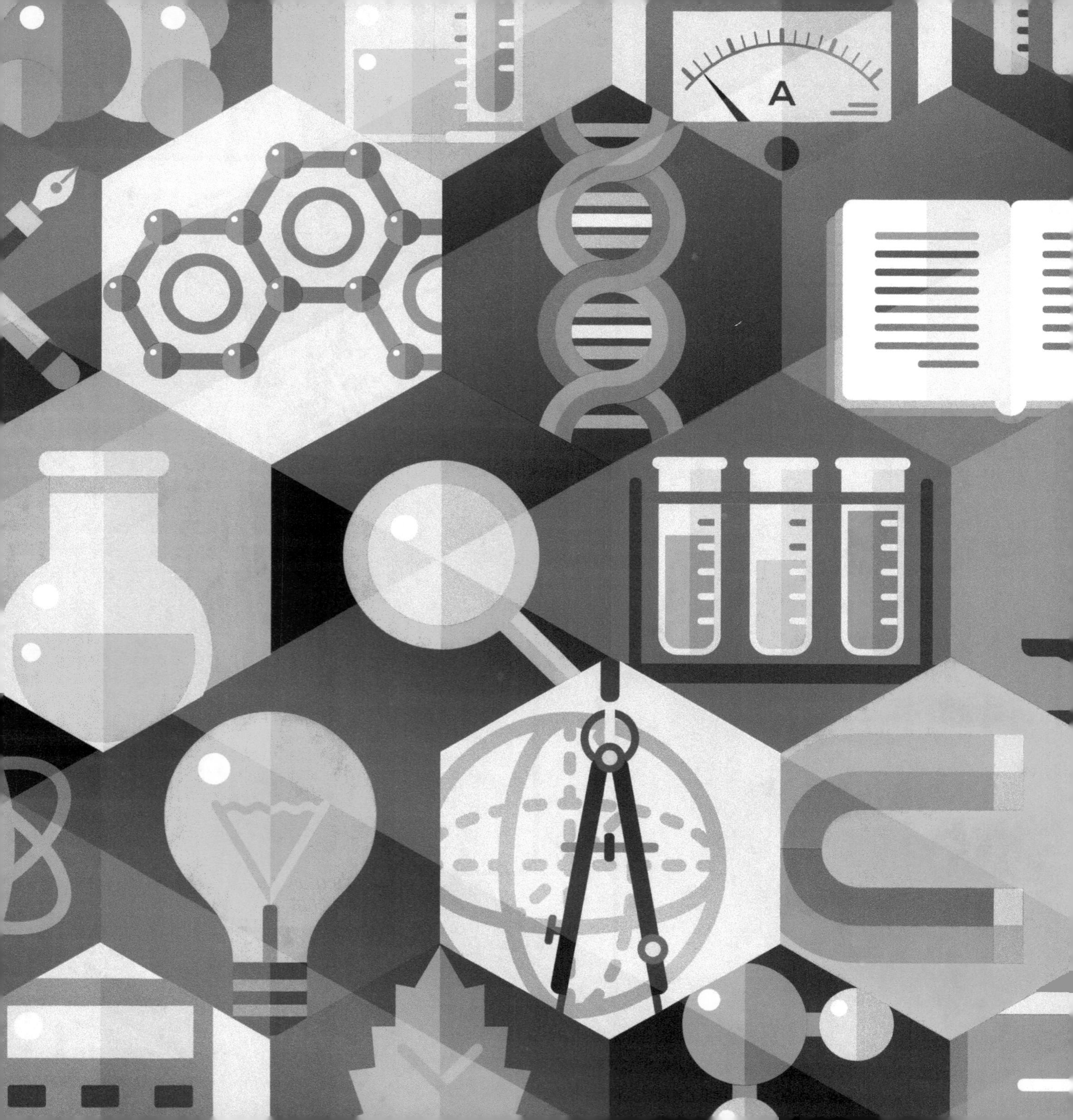
A

HOOKE'S MICROGRAPHIA

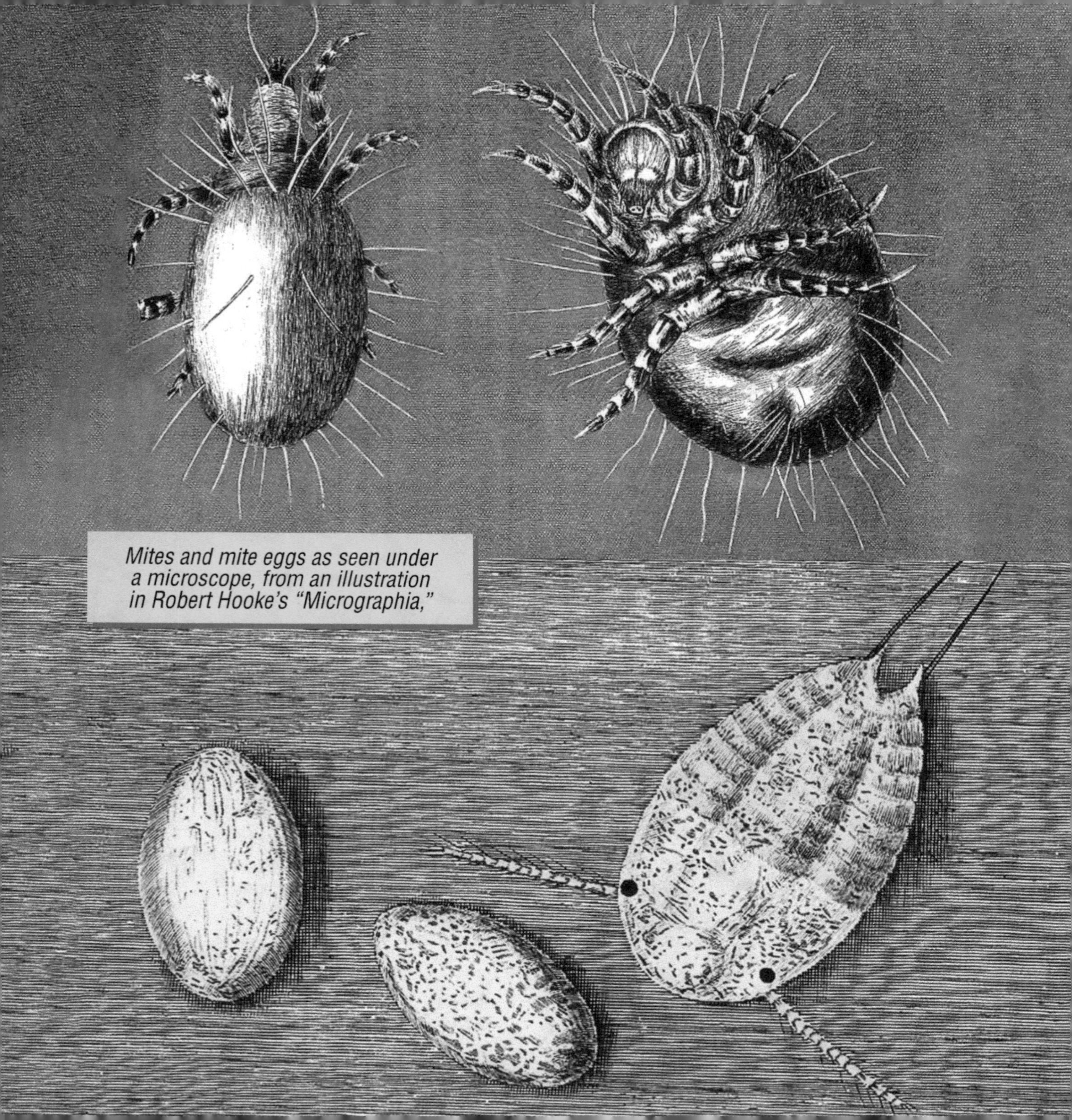

Mites and mite eggs as seen under a microscope, from an illustration in Robert Hooke's "Micrographia,"

Hooke's *Micrographia* was to become one of the most influential books ever penned because it brought to light an entirely new, previously unseen world. Today's knowledge in the fields of microbiology, as well as in the fields of quantum physics and the growing field of nanotechnology might never have existed if it hadn't been for Hooke's inspiring drawings. They awakened the desire to pursue further discoveries in the micro-world.

As he continued to make new discoveries with his light microscope, Hooke discovered microscopic fungi. This was in 1665, nine years before Anton van Leeuwenhoek's discovery of life forms that were composed of single cells.

Anton van Leeuwenhoek

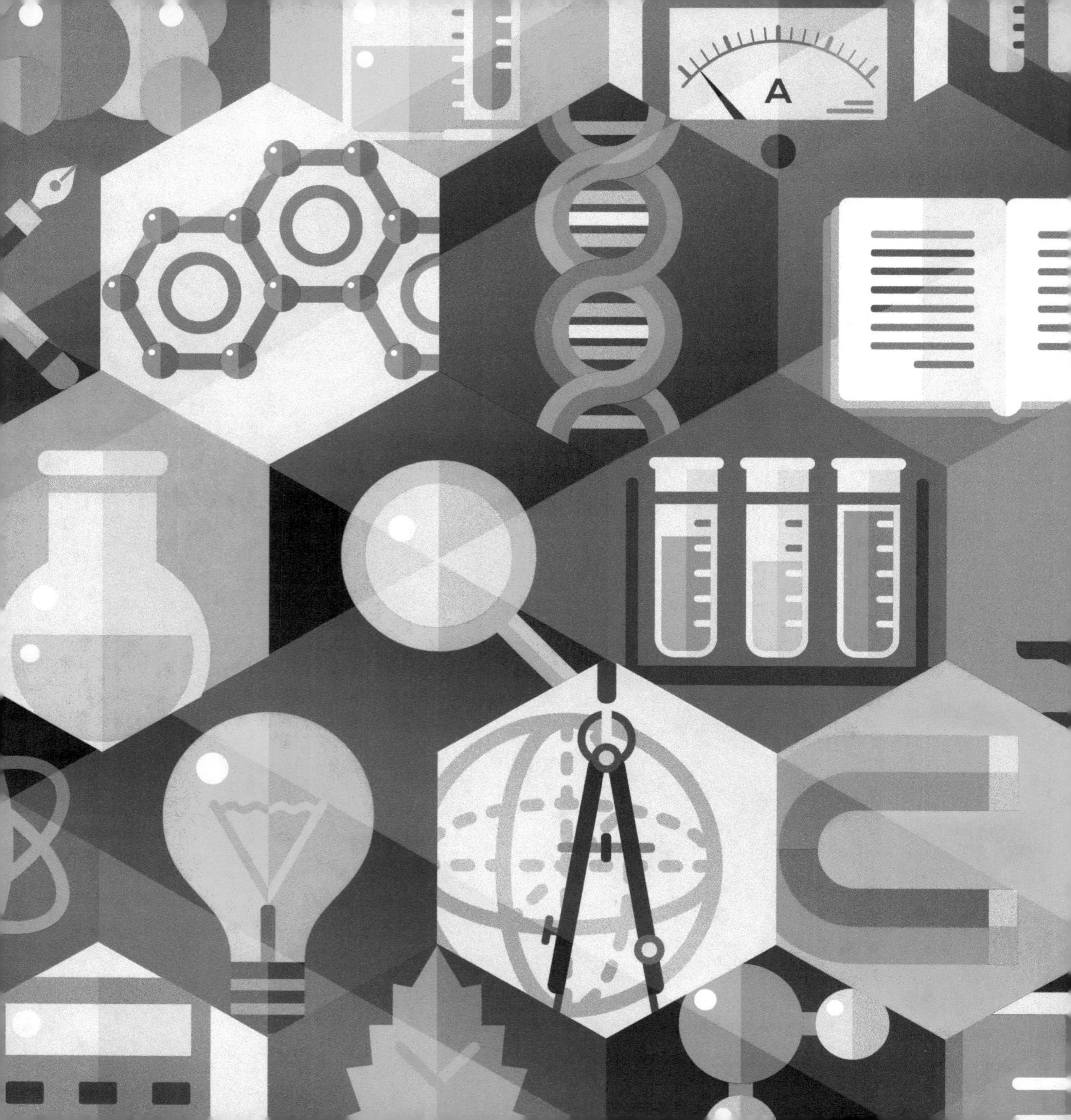
A

HOOKE OBSERVES THE STRUCTURE OF PLANTS

A cork tree's bark detail

Another specimen that Hooke observed was from a cork tree's bark. The pattern he discovered and sketched made him think about the individual dwelling areas inside a monastery, which were called cellula. He coined the name "cells" to describe them. He didn't realize the true nature or function of cells because the cells he was viewing were dead cells. They no longer contained the structures that living cells have, such as a nucleus and other organelles.

The structure of cork as viewed under a microscope when cut lengthwise (left) and crosswise, showing the 'cellulae' with walls bounding the 'cells'

The first person to view a living cell with a microscope was Leeuwenhoek. In 1674, he observed Spirogyra, a form of algae. It's likely that he also observed different types of bacteria.

Spirogyra structure

GREEN ALGAE

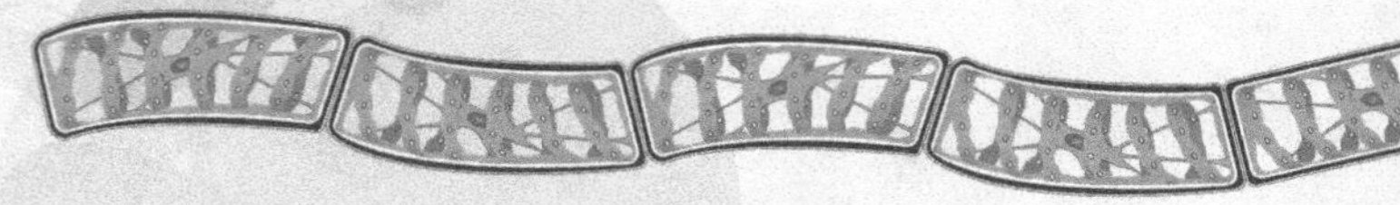

SPIROGYRA

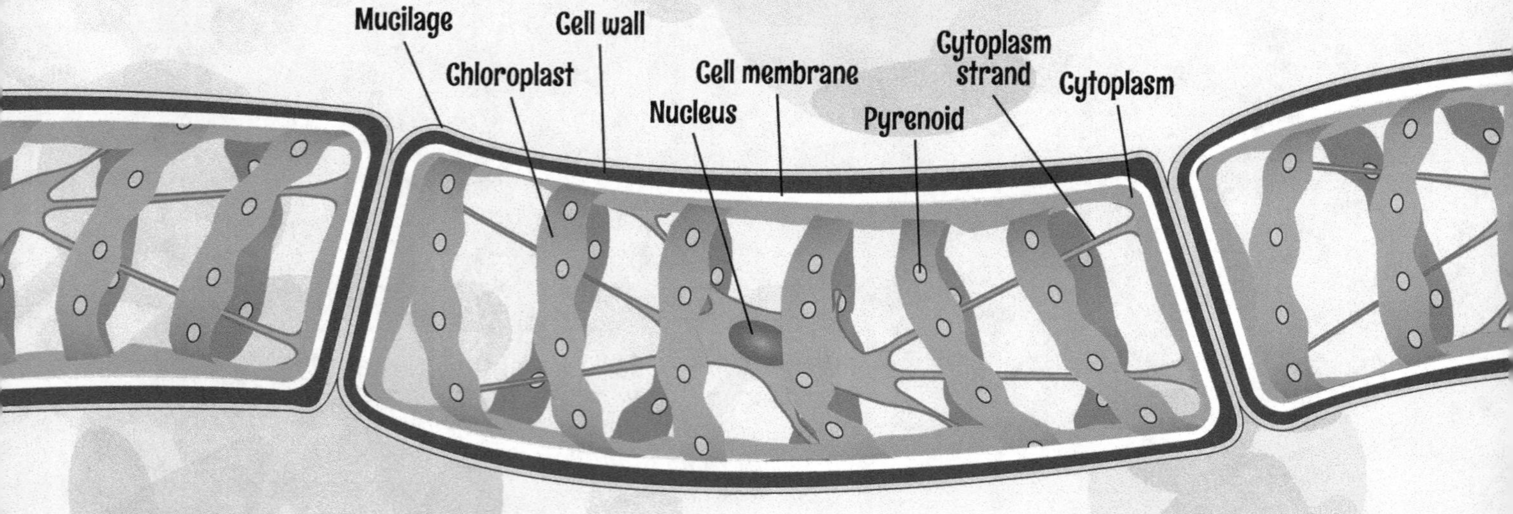

Green Spirogyra is a fresh water algae

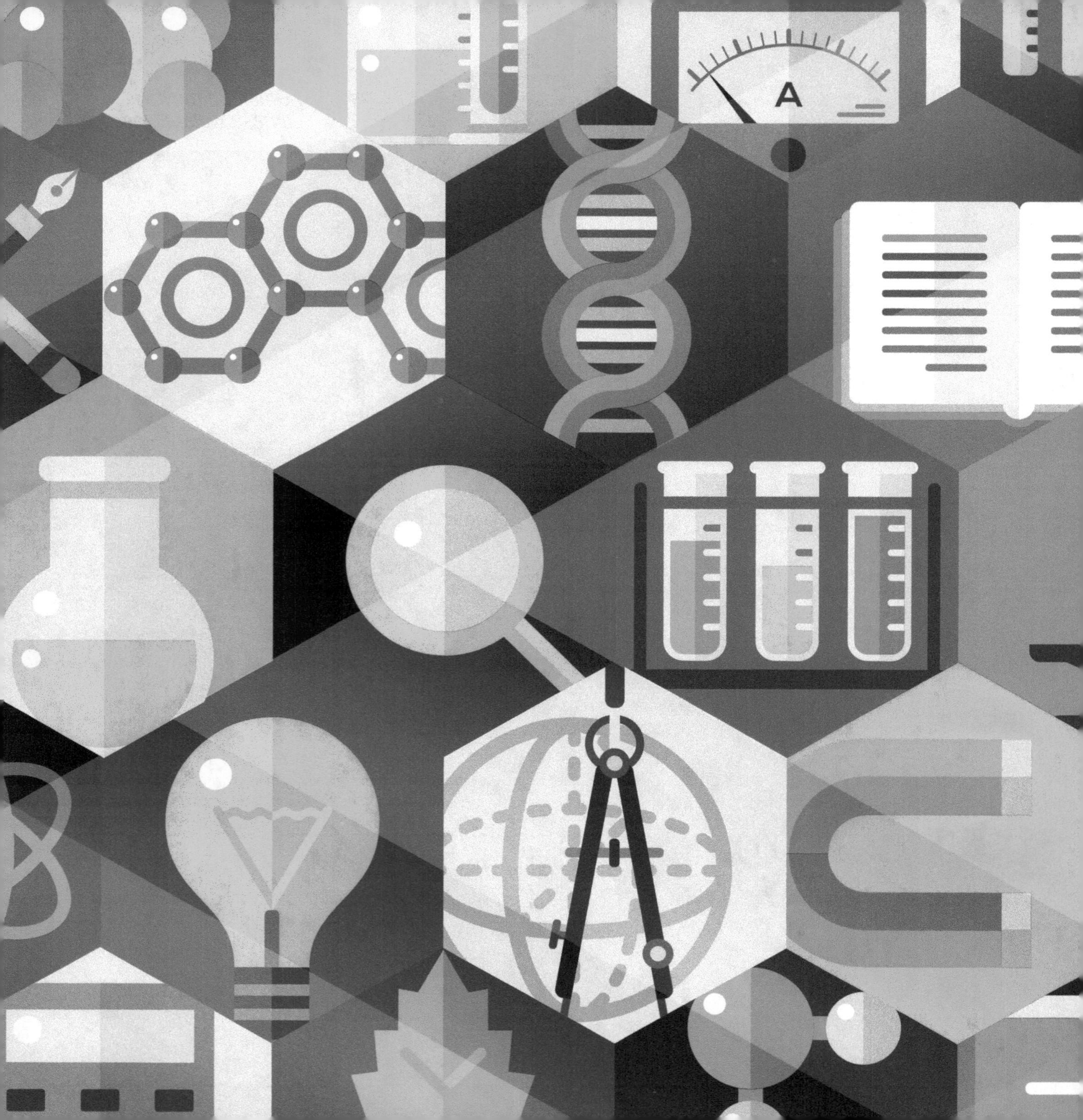
A

WHO FORMULATED THE PRINCIPLES OF CELL THEORY?

ANIMAL CELL ANATOMY

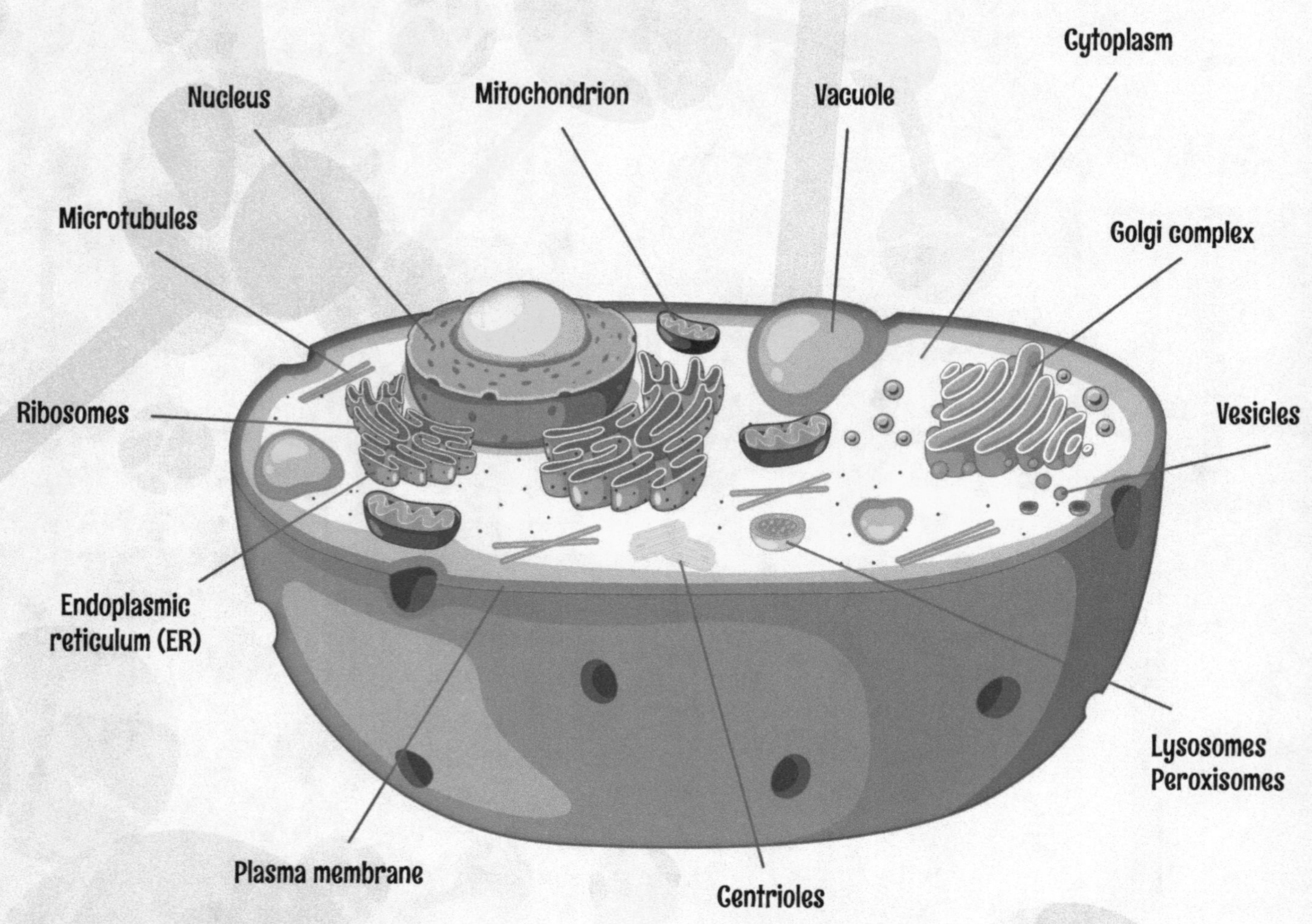

In 1838, Theodor Schwann and his colleague Matthias Schleiden were having coffee after dinner and comparing their scientific notes on cells. As Schwann listened to Schleiden's description of the composition of the nuclei of plant cells he was suddenly aware of how similar these cells seemed to be in comparison to the animal cells he was studying.

Theodor Schwann

Matthias Schleiden

The two colleagues stopped what they were doing and went to the lab to observe Schwann's slides. The following year Schwann published his essay on animal and plant cells. He made three important summaries about cells. The first two tenets were correct, but the third was incorrect.

PLANT CELL ANATOMY

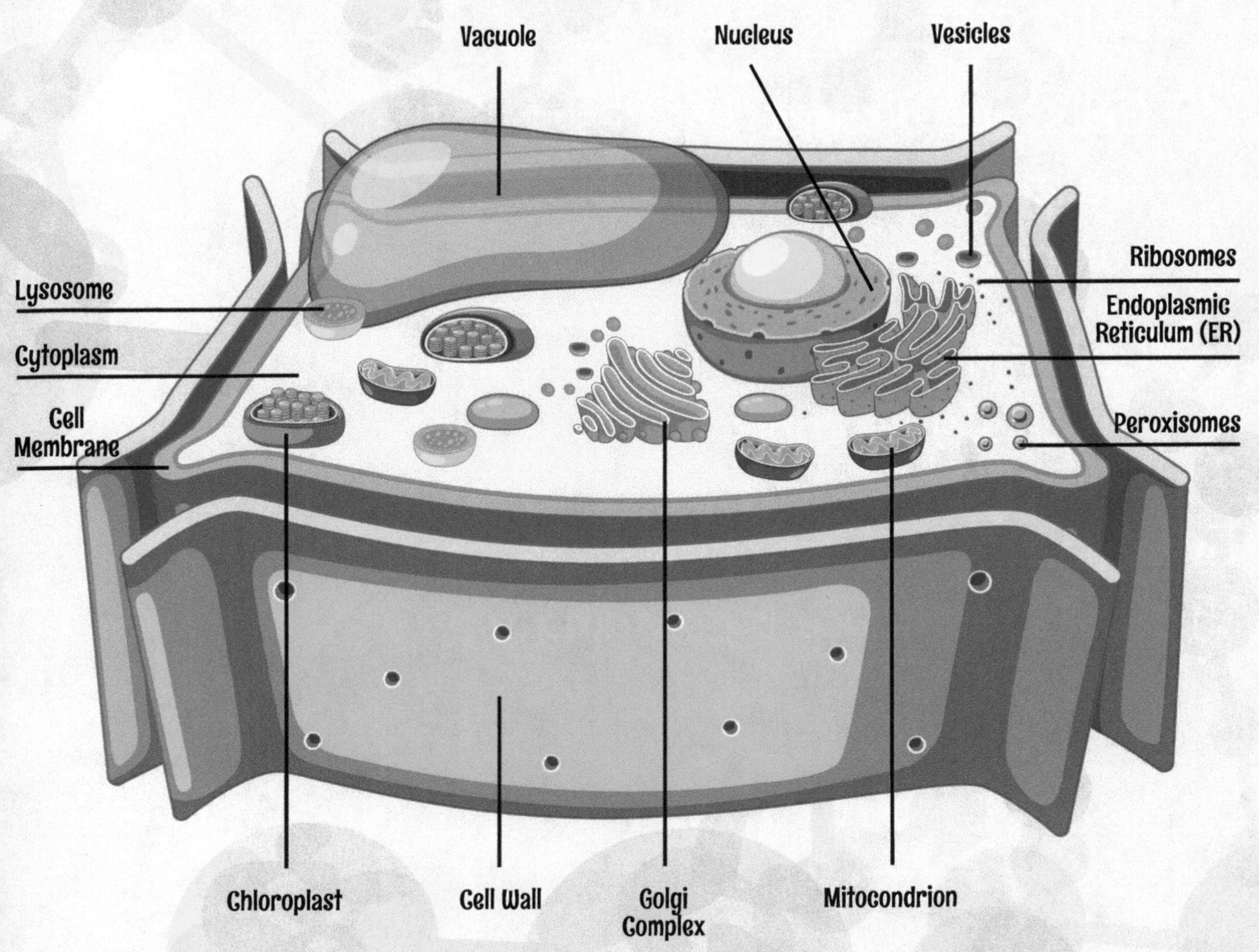

1. Cells are the structural units of all living organisms.
2. Cells are distinct entities, but they are also the 'building blocks' that compose living tissues.
3. Cells form in a similar way as mineral crystals. This conjecture was false.

Eventually, other scientists discovered that cells reproduce by dividing.

Scientists discovered that cells reproduce by dividing

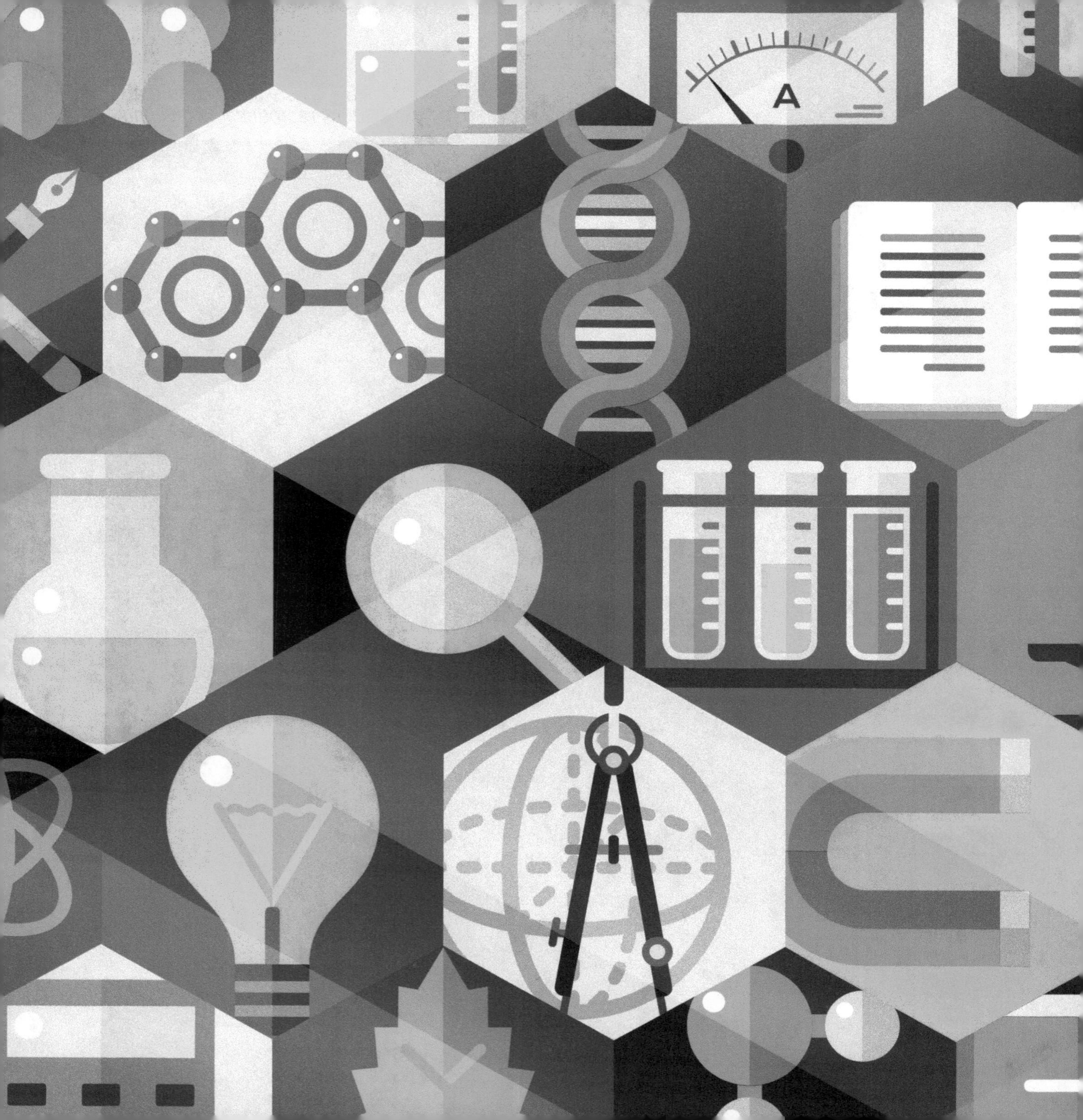
A

RUDOLF VIRCHOW'S CONTRIBUTIONS TO MODERN CELL THEORY

In 1858, Rudolf Virchow was studying cells with microscopes that were much more sophisticated than the ones that Hooke had previously used. His observations led him to believe that cells were only able to come from other living cells. For example, when a single-celled organism gets larger, it eventually divides to create new cells.

Rudolf Virchow

In other words, cells can only be formed by pre-existing cells. Your body is making new cells all the time, but in every case the new cells that are being formed come from existing cells. Virchow's hypothesis led to these three important principles that are the foundation of modern biology.

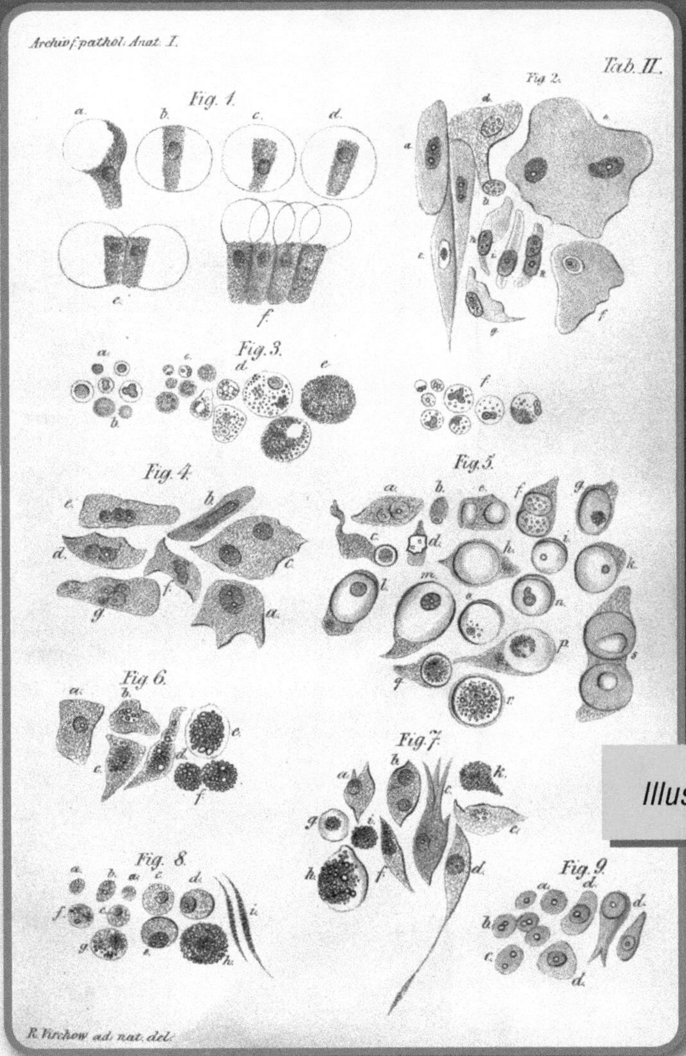

Illustration of Virchow's cell theory

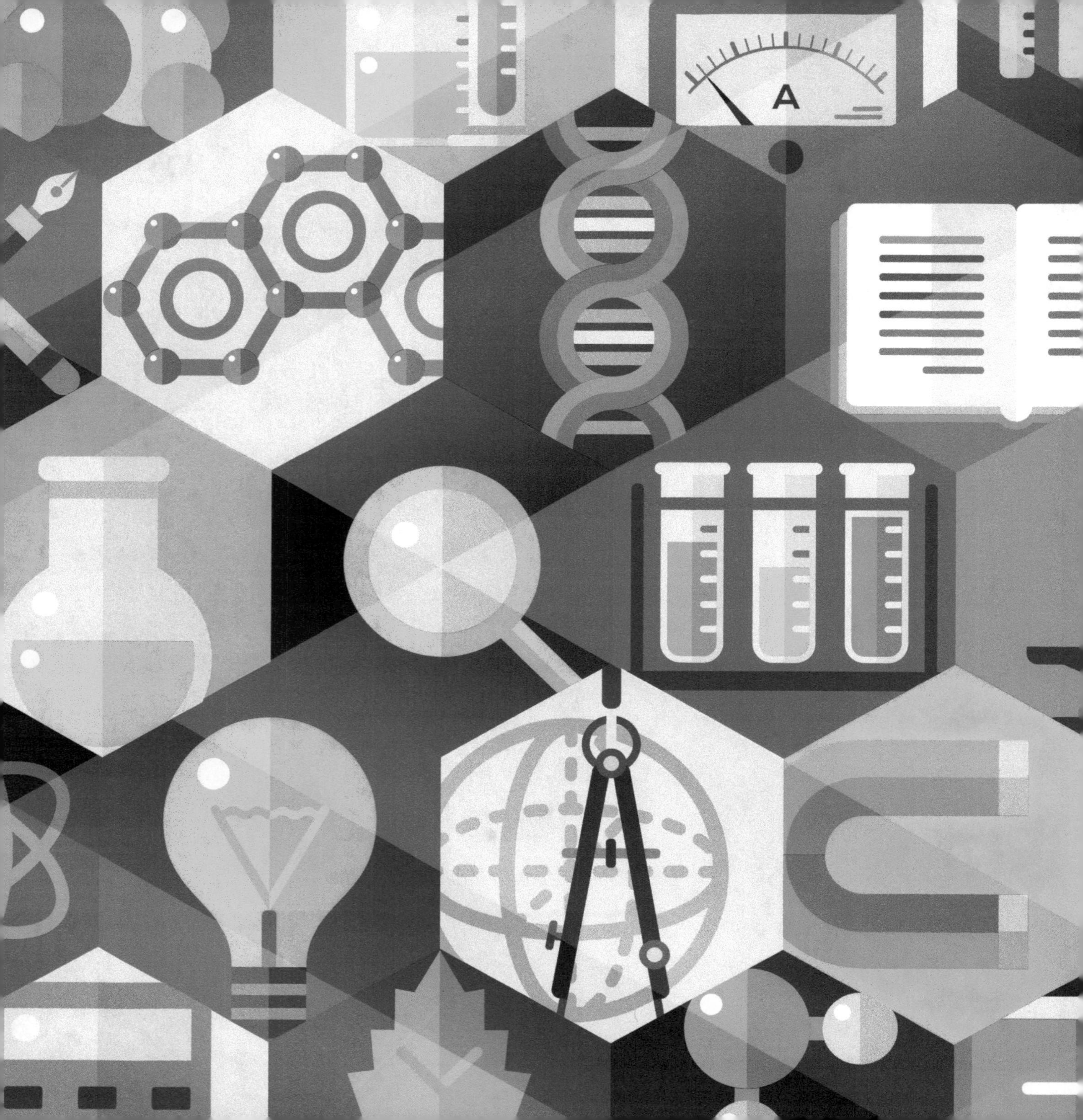
A

MODERN CELL THEORY

1. All living organisms on Earth are made up of cells.
2. Living cells make up the basic structure and organization of all living organisms.
3. New cells come from other cells that are alive and have grown large enough to divide. In other words, cell division creates new cells. New cells don't generate spontaneously or form like inanimate crystals.

After Virchow formulated his theory, thousands of experiments underscored that he was correct. To date, no evidence has surfaced to contradict his theory, so his principles are the core of biological science.

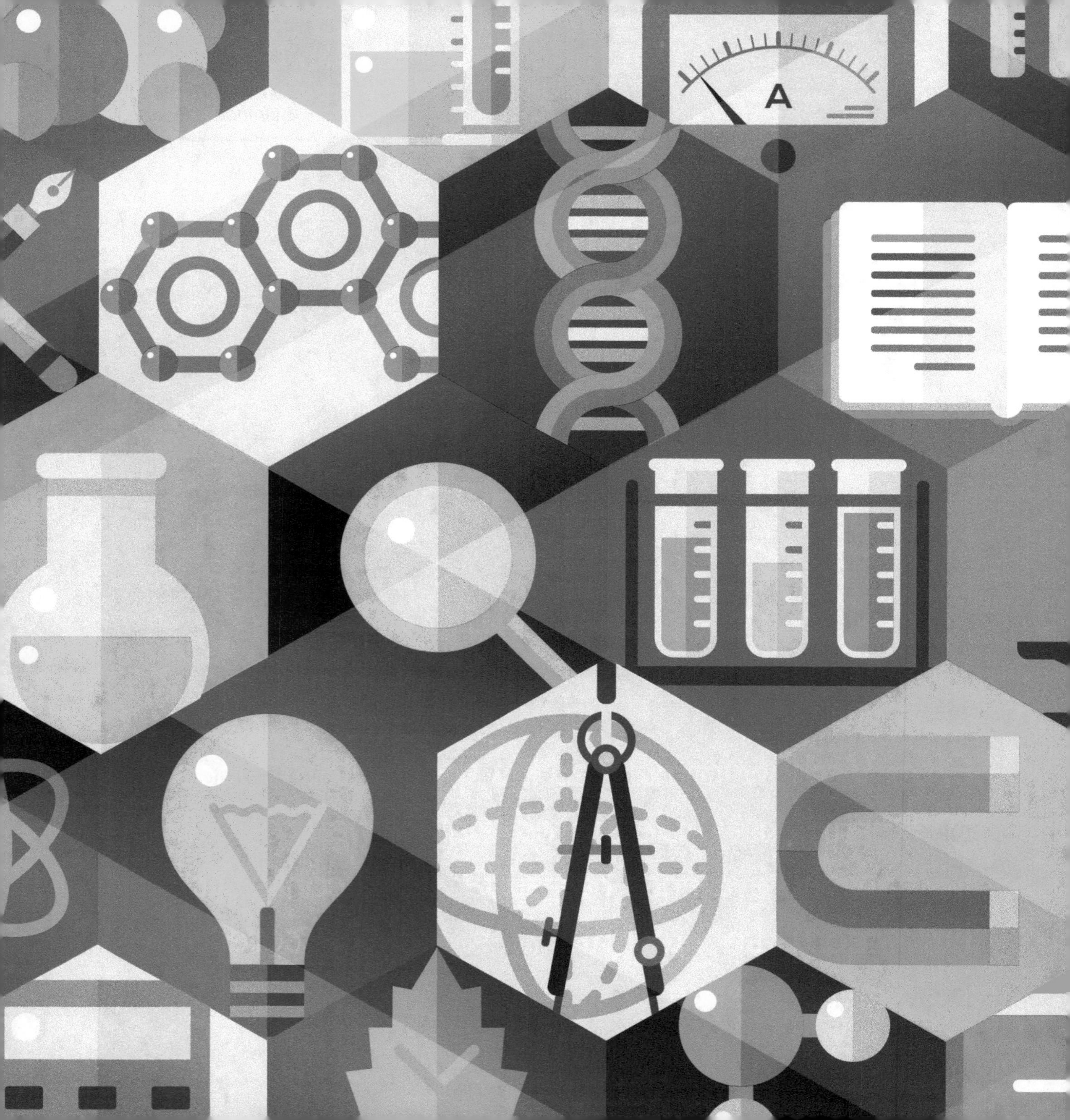
A

ELECTRON MICROSCOPES ARE INVENTED

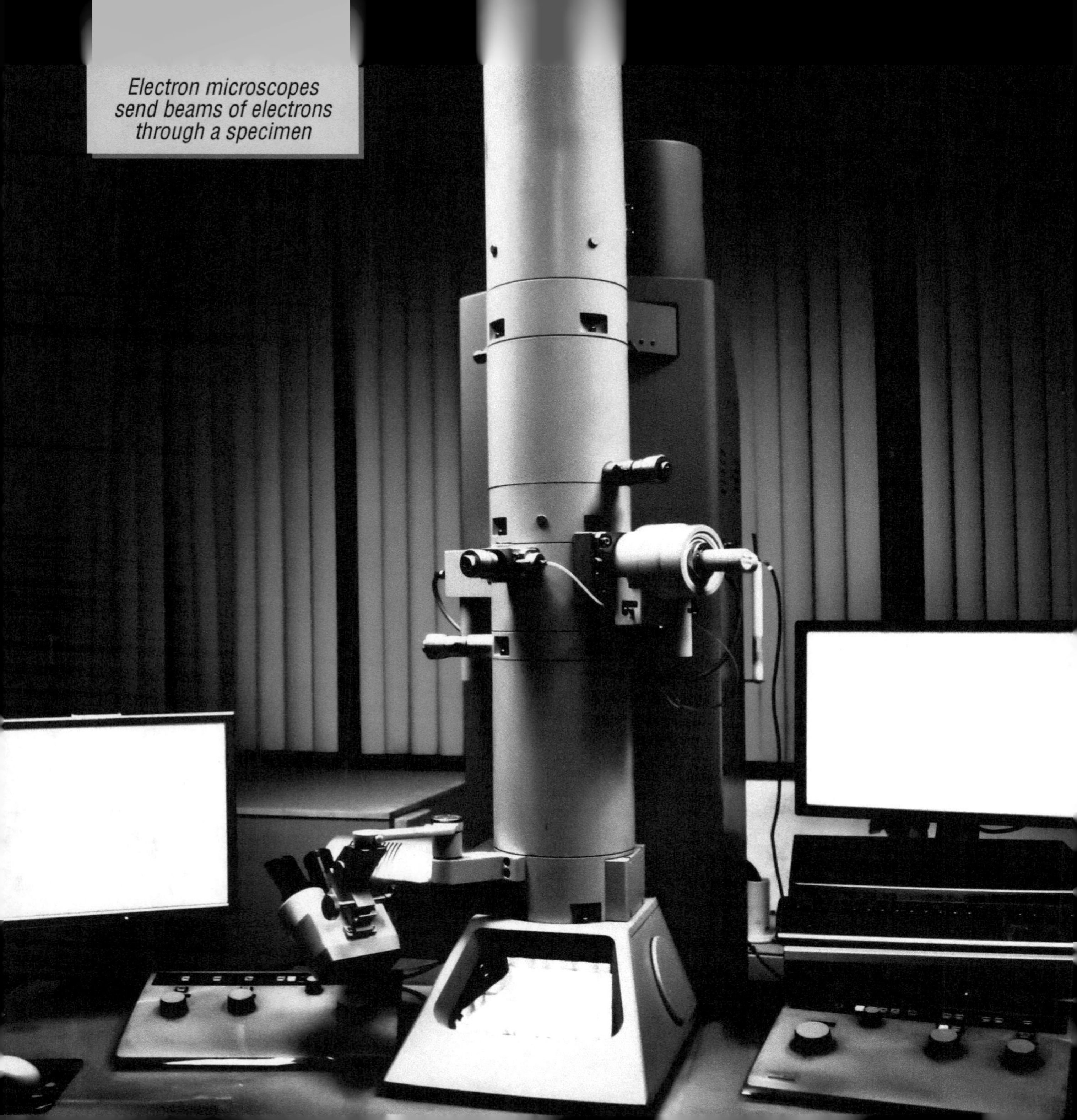

Electron microscopes send beams of electrons through a specimen

Scientists invented microscopes that were more powerful in the 1950s. These microscopes were called electron microscopes. These types of microscopes differ in the way they work compared to a light microscope, which is the type of microscope that Hooke used. Instead of using beams of light, electron microscopes send beams of electrons through a specimen.

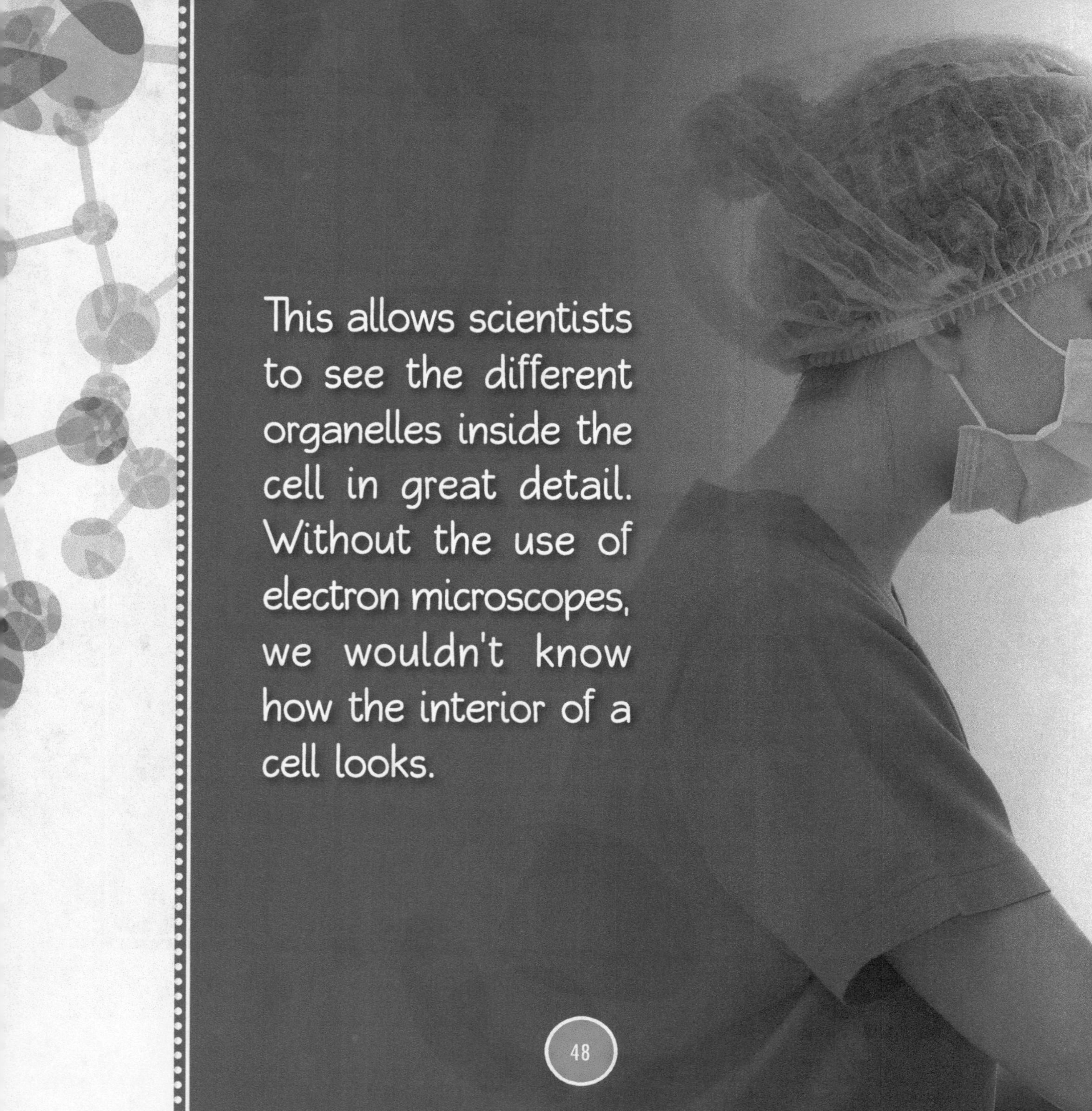

This allows scientists to see the different organelles inside the cell in great detail. Without the use of electron microscopes, we wouldn't know how the interior of a cell looks.

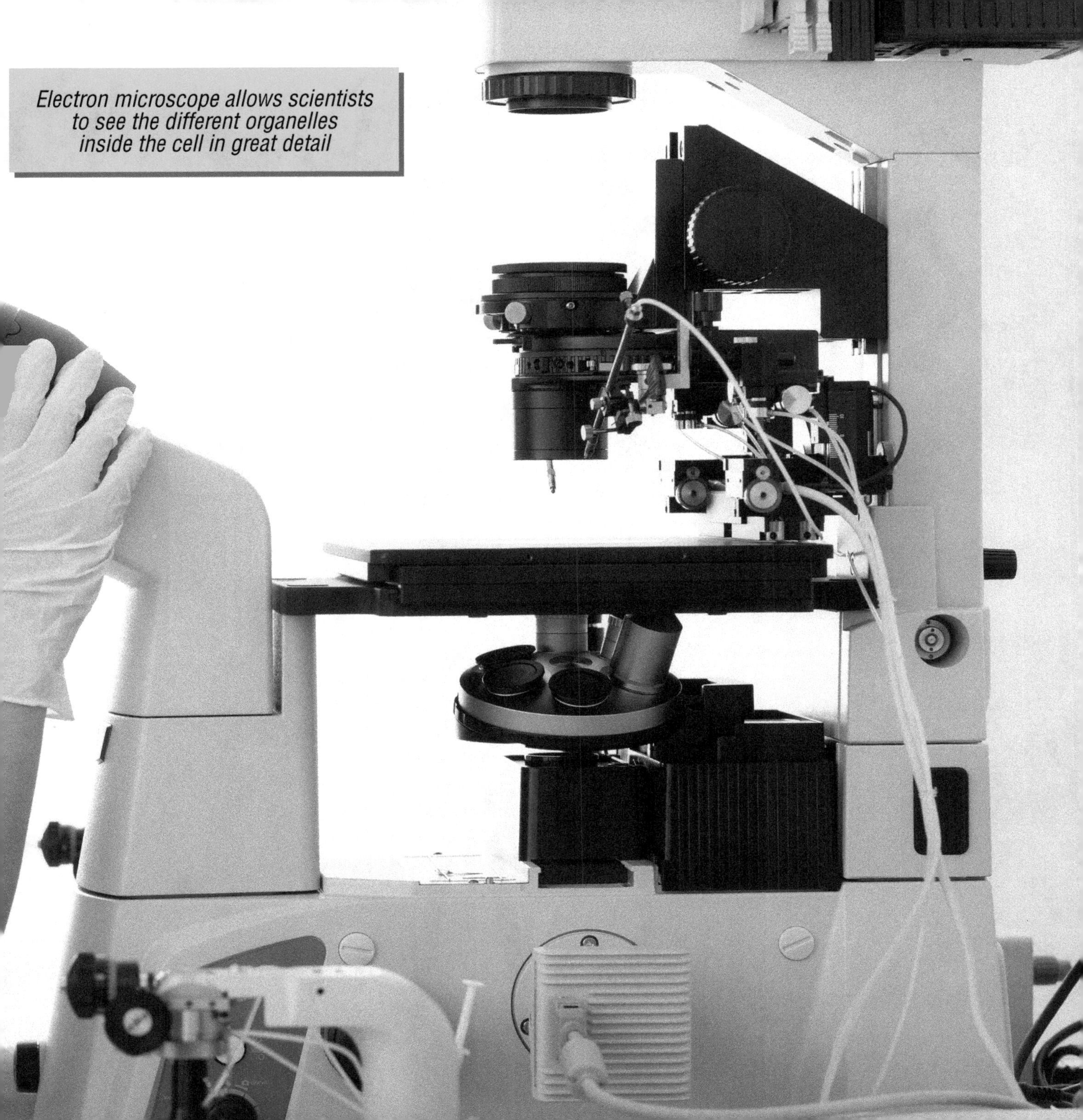
Electron microscope allows scientists to see the different organelles inside the cell in great detail

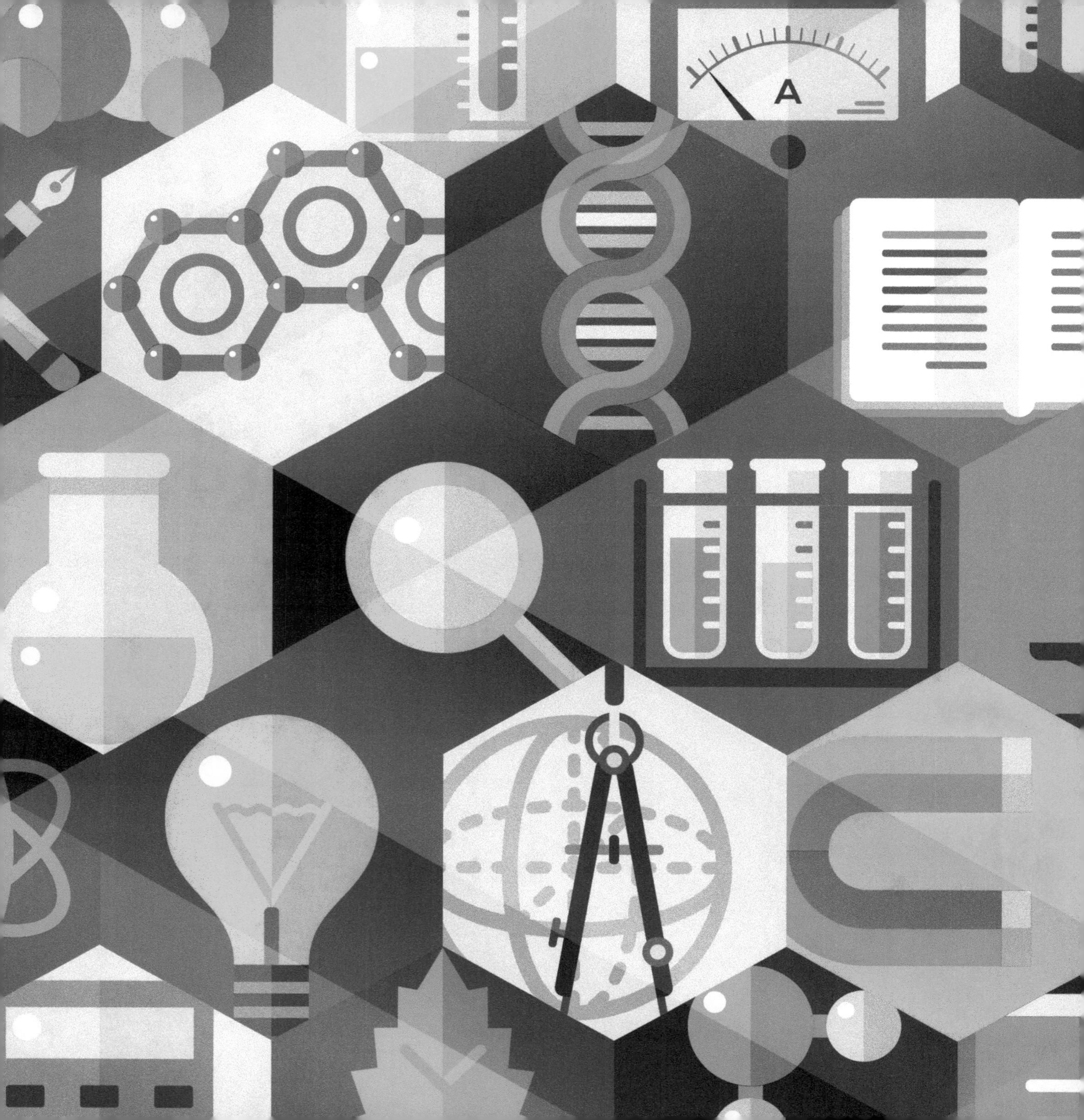
A

ONE CELL OR TRILLIONS OF CELLS?

The living organisms on Earth vary from single-celled organisms to complex, multicellular organisms such as humans. Human bodies contain trillions of cells. When you see pictures of cells in textbooks, they show the basic parts of both animal and plant cells, but what isn't often discussed is that the cells in our bodies come in all different sizes as well as shapes. These different sizes and shapes have to do with the various functions the cells have.

CELLS OF THE HUMAN BODY

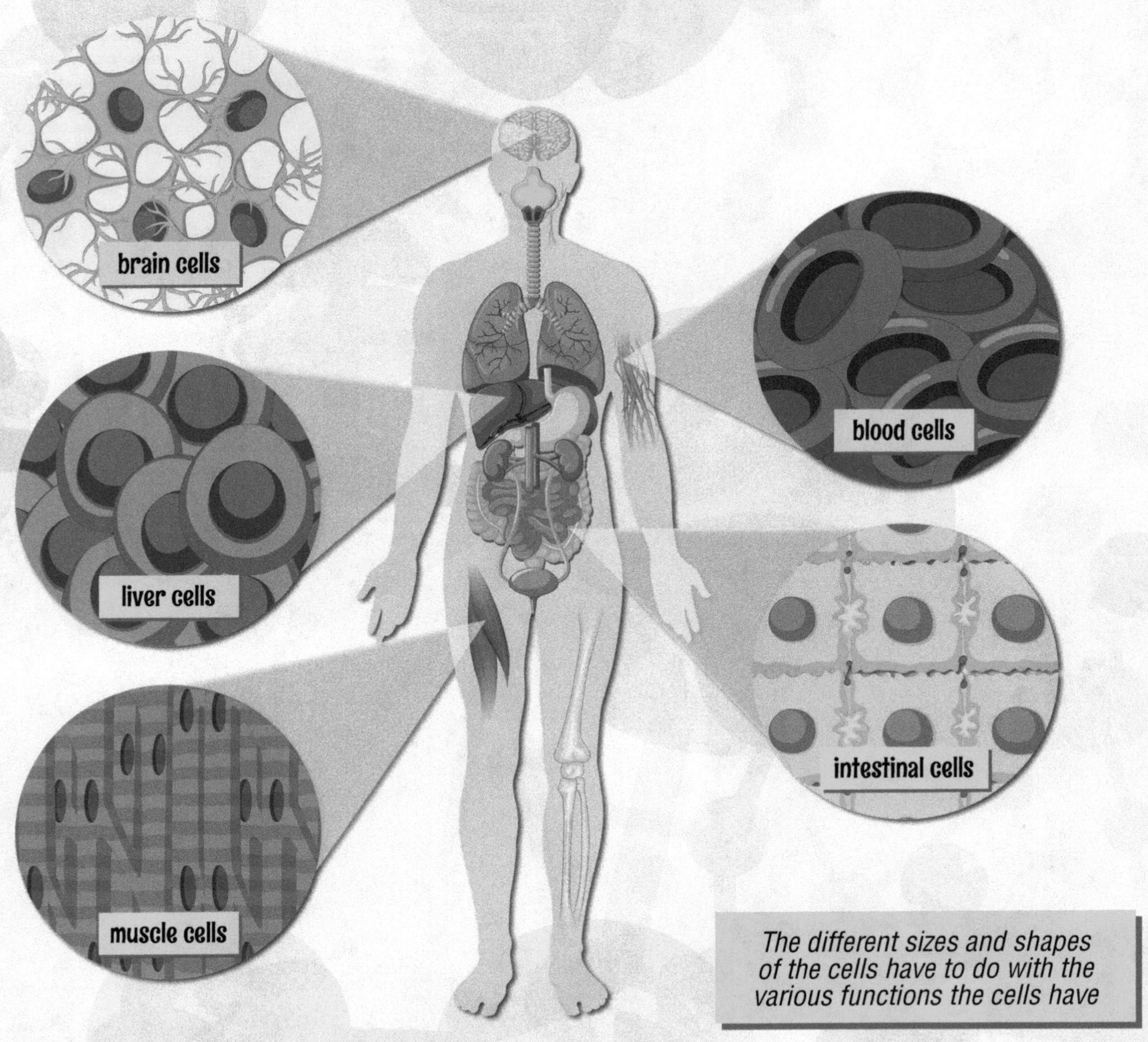

The different sizes and shapes of the cells have to do with the various functions the cells have

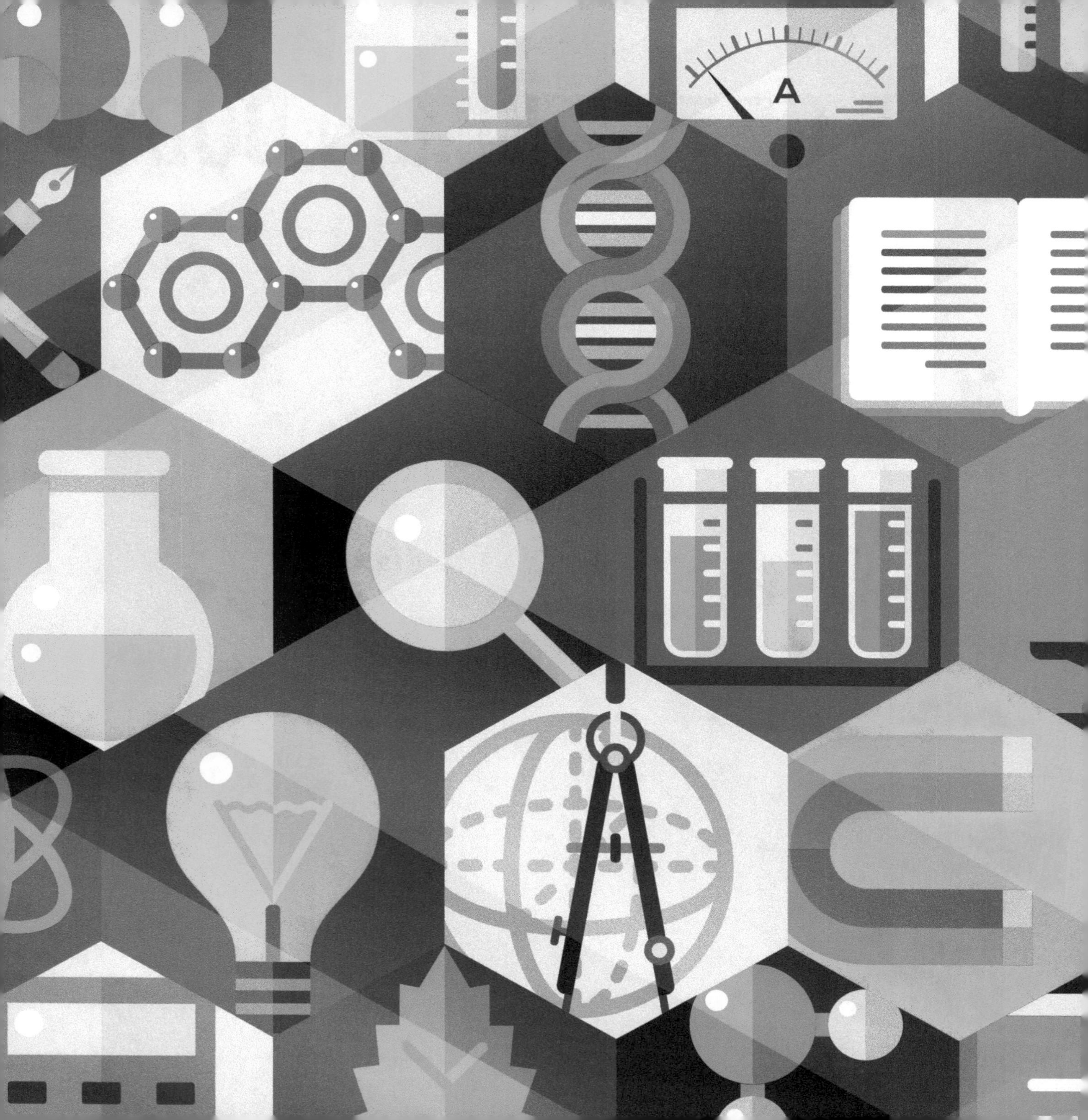
A

HUMAN CELLS ARE SPECIALIZED

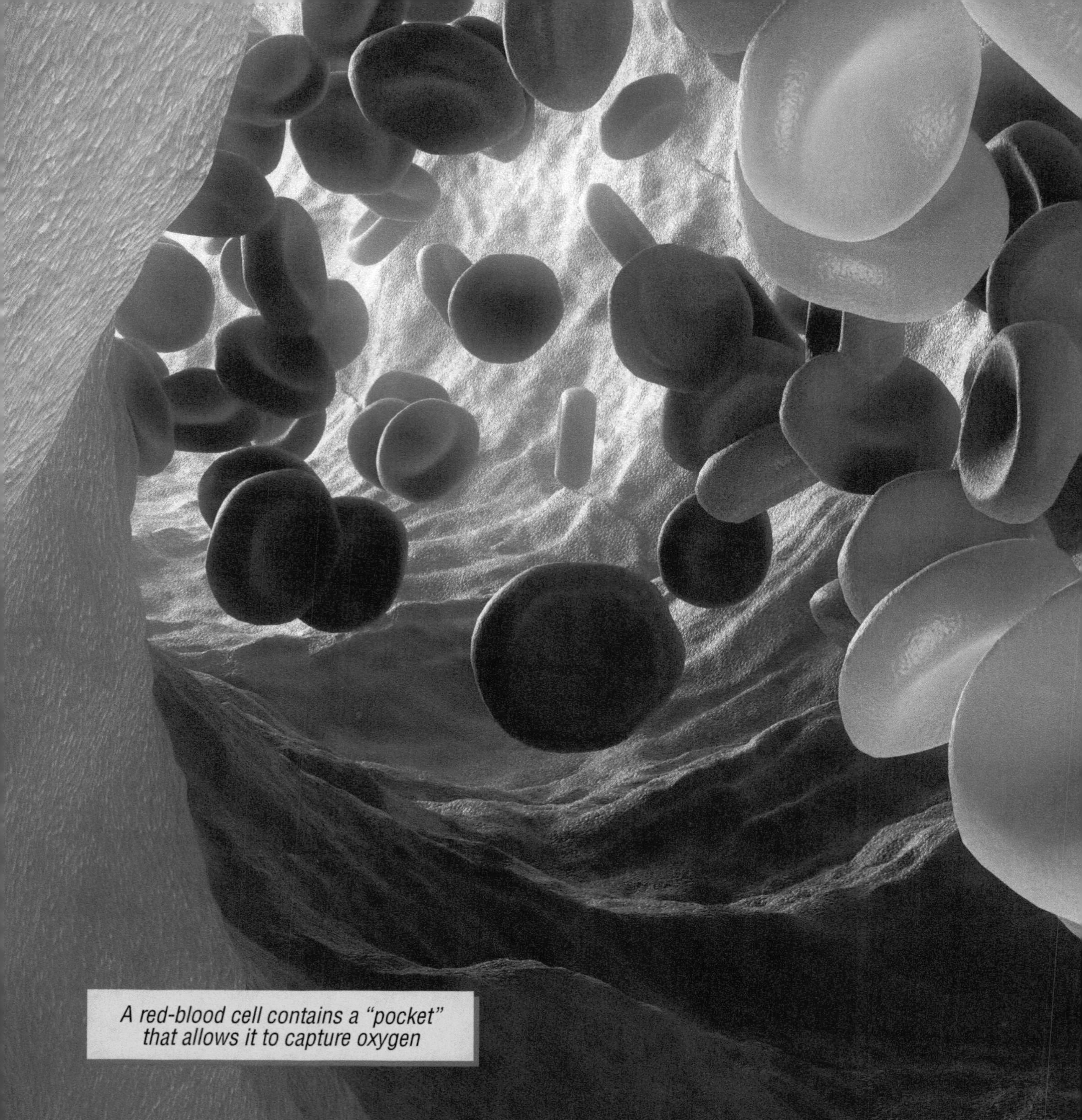
A red-blood cell contains a "pocket" that allows it to capture oxygen

Each cell in the human body has a specific role to play in the body's processes. For example, if you observed a red-blood cell, you would see that it contains a "pocket" that allows it to capture oxygen so that it can transport it to other cells.

Another example is nerve cells, which are called neurons. These types of cells form communication lines throughout the body. They are stringy and long, which is reminiscent of a wire. This long, stringy shape helps them to move messages and signals to the command center, your brain, very quickly. If you touch something hot, the nerve cells recognize it as potentially dangerous and immediately send a signal to your brain.

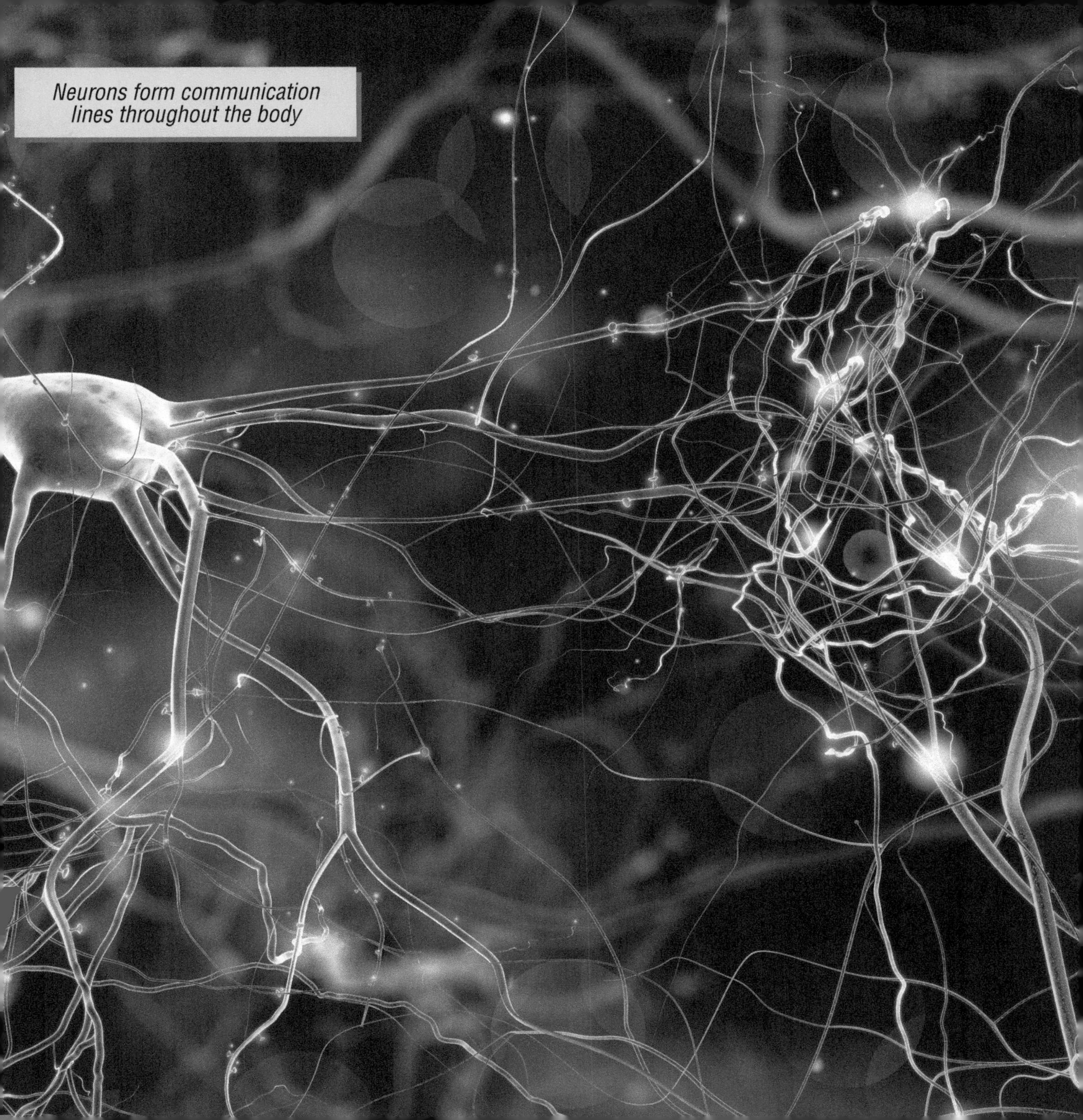

Neurons form communication lines throughout the body

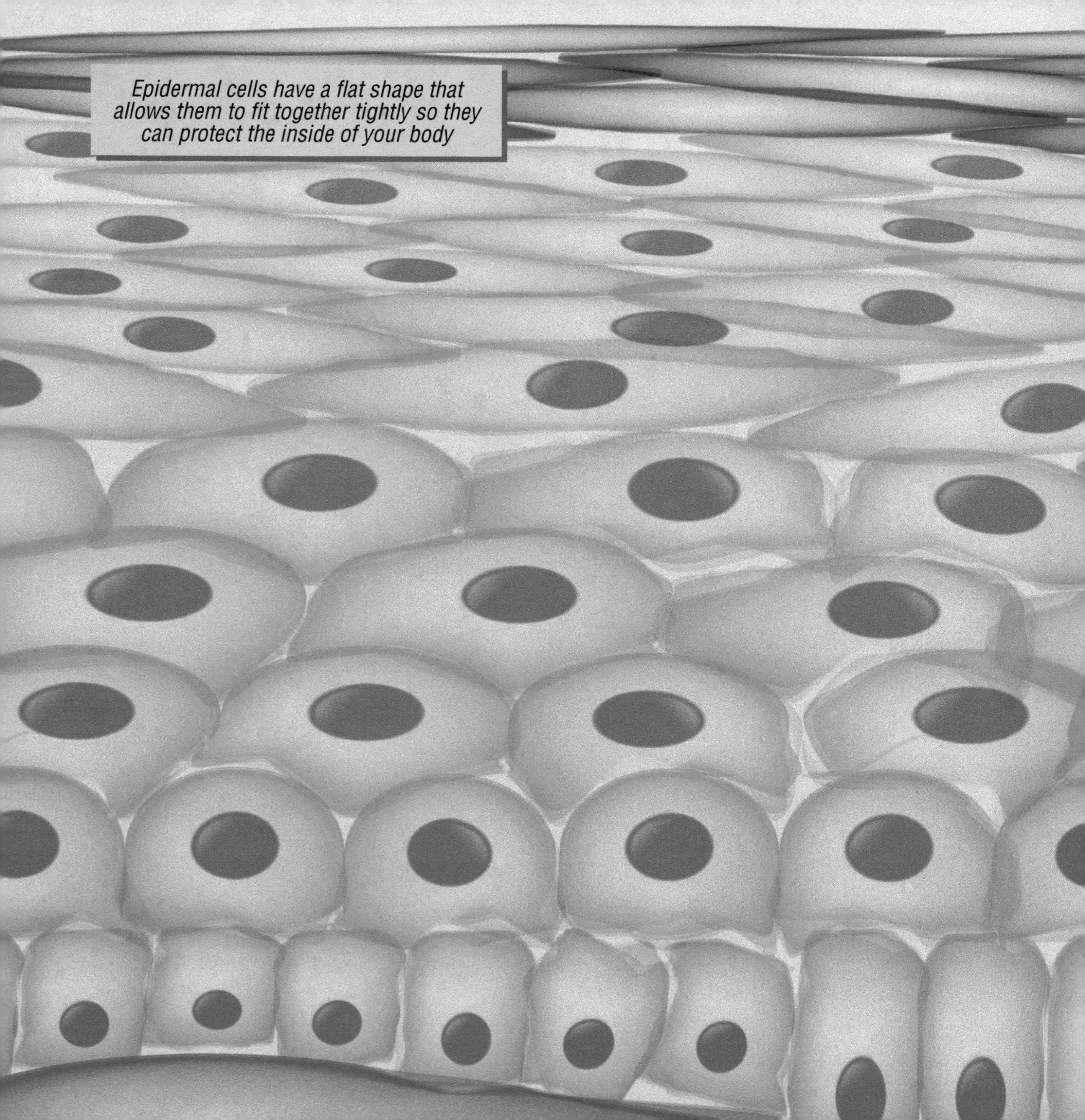

Epidermal cells have a flat shape that allows them to fit together tightly so they can protect the inside of your body

If you examine your skin cells, also called epidermal cells, you would see that they have a flat shape that allows them to fit together tightly so they can protect the inside of your body. There are many different types of specialized cells within our bodies as there are with all many-celled organisms.

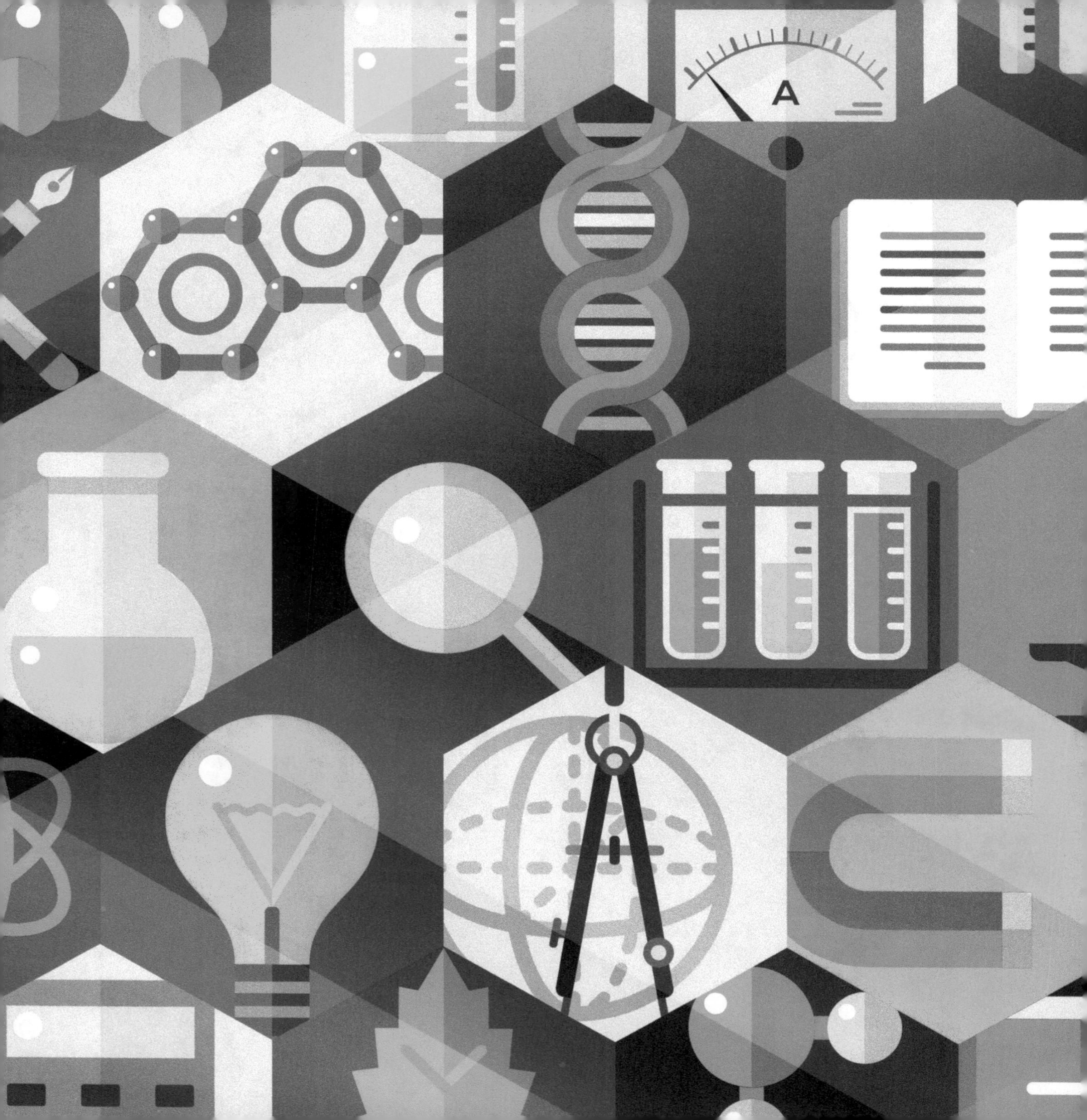
A

ORGANIZATIONAL LEVELS OF CELLS, TISSUES, AND ORGANS

STOMACH TISSUES

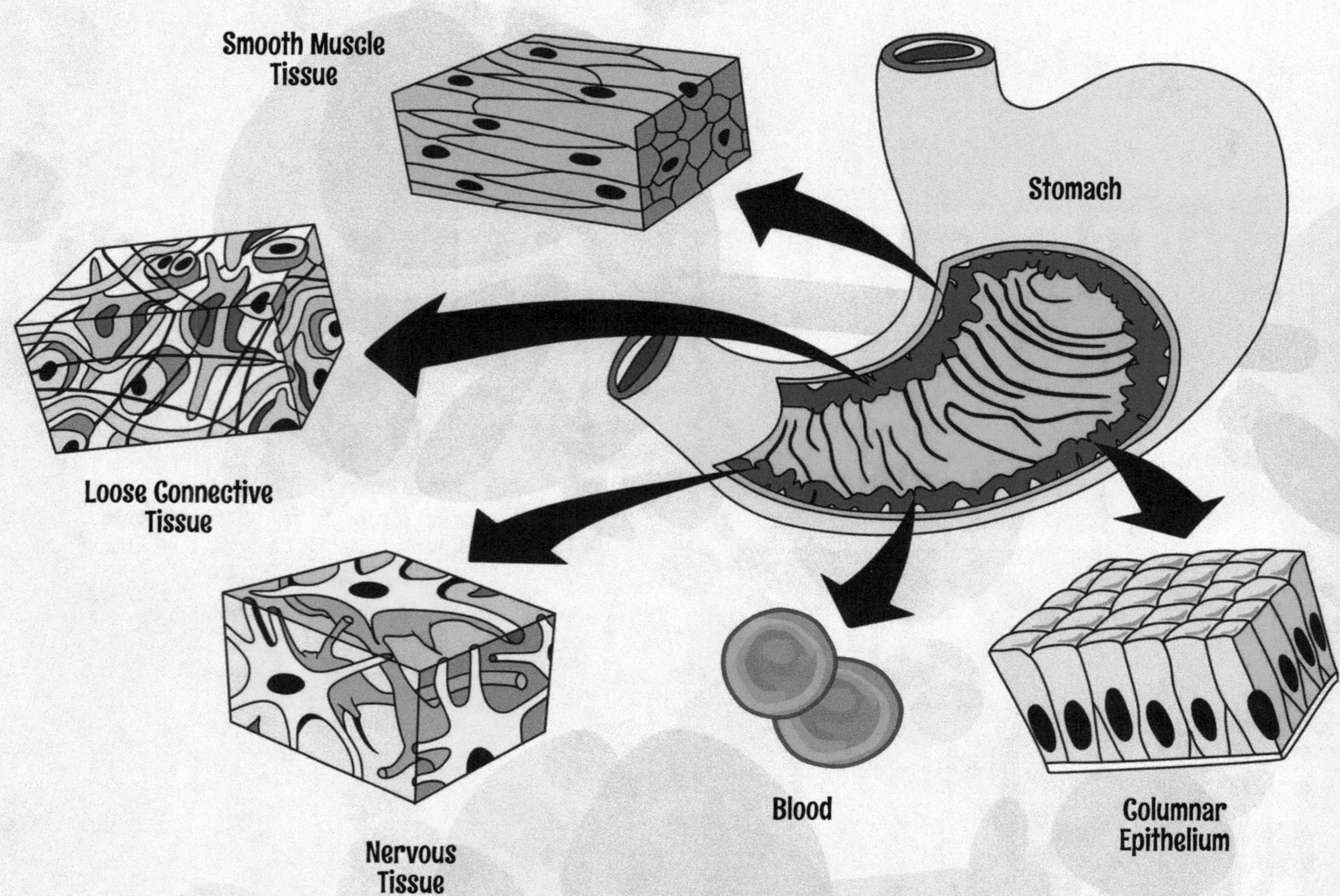

The tissues of your stomach are composed of stomach cells

Even though cells are the basic building blocks of organisms, cells organize into groups to perform a specific role together. These specialized cells are arranged as living tissue. For example, the tissues of your stomach are composed of stomach cells. The stomach tissues are connected in such a way that they make up the organ of your stomach. Within your organs, there are two or more types of tissues. These tissues are specialized to work in tandem with each other to perform the job that particular organ does, which is, in this case, to digest your food.

HUMAN BODY ORGAN SYSTEMS

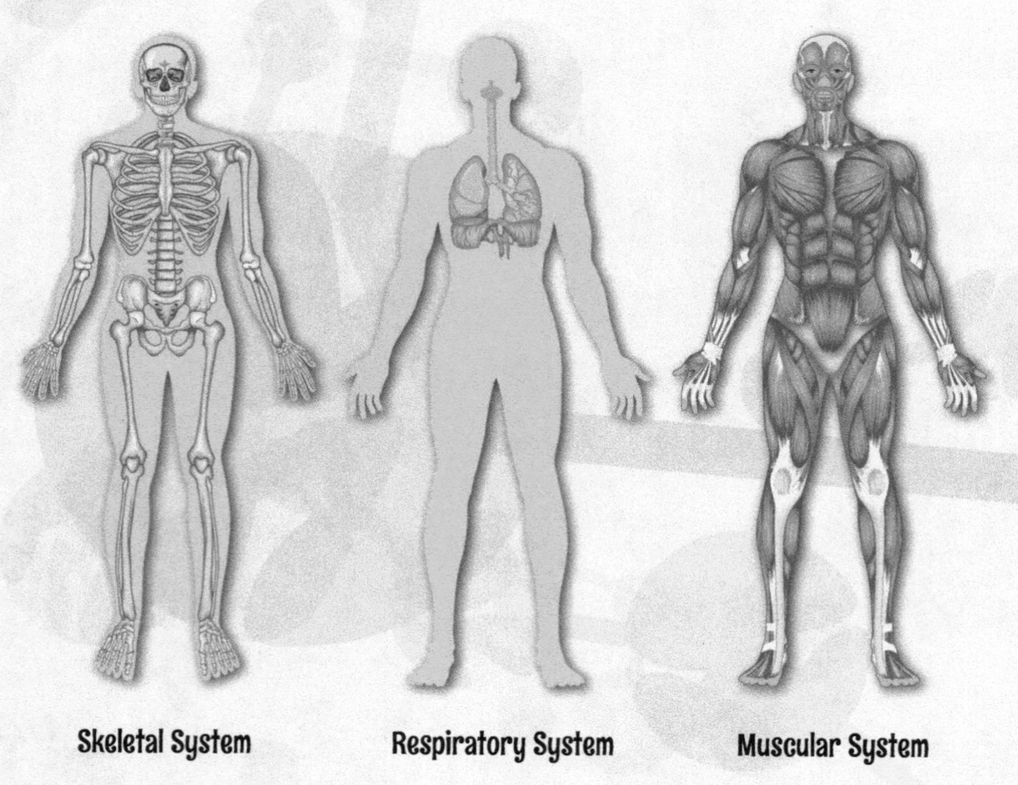

Cells build tissues and tissues build organs. Organs are arranged into systems of organs. For example, your spinal cord and your nerves form a network with your brain that forms your nervous system. Your nervous system works with other organ systems such as your digestive system or your circulatory system. Each of these systems has organs that are connected to each other and are made up of specialized tissues and specialized cells.

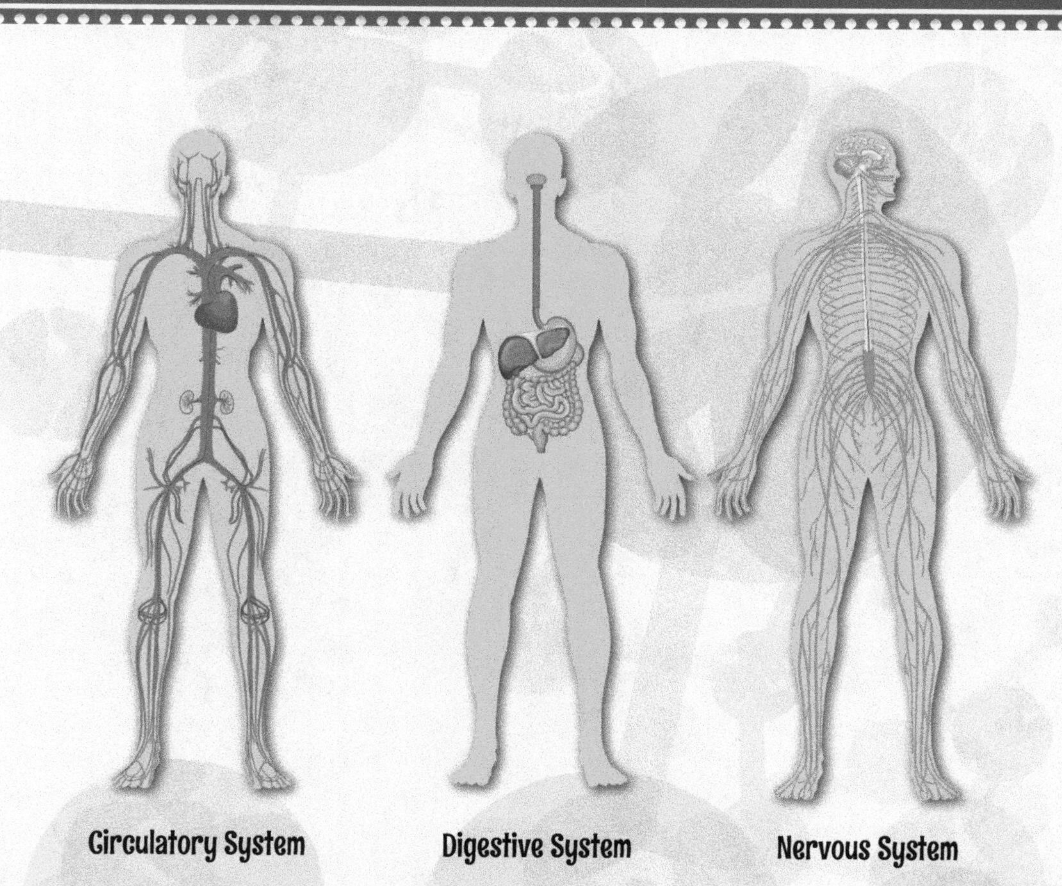

What's even more amazing is that cells are constructed from chemical atoms and molecules, which are not living materials. The size of an atom compared to the size of a cell is similar to a marble inside a house. There are trillions of atoms in just one living cell! Today, we have electron microscopes that allow us to view atoms and atomic structures.

There are trillions of atoms in just one living cell

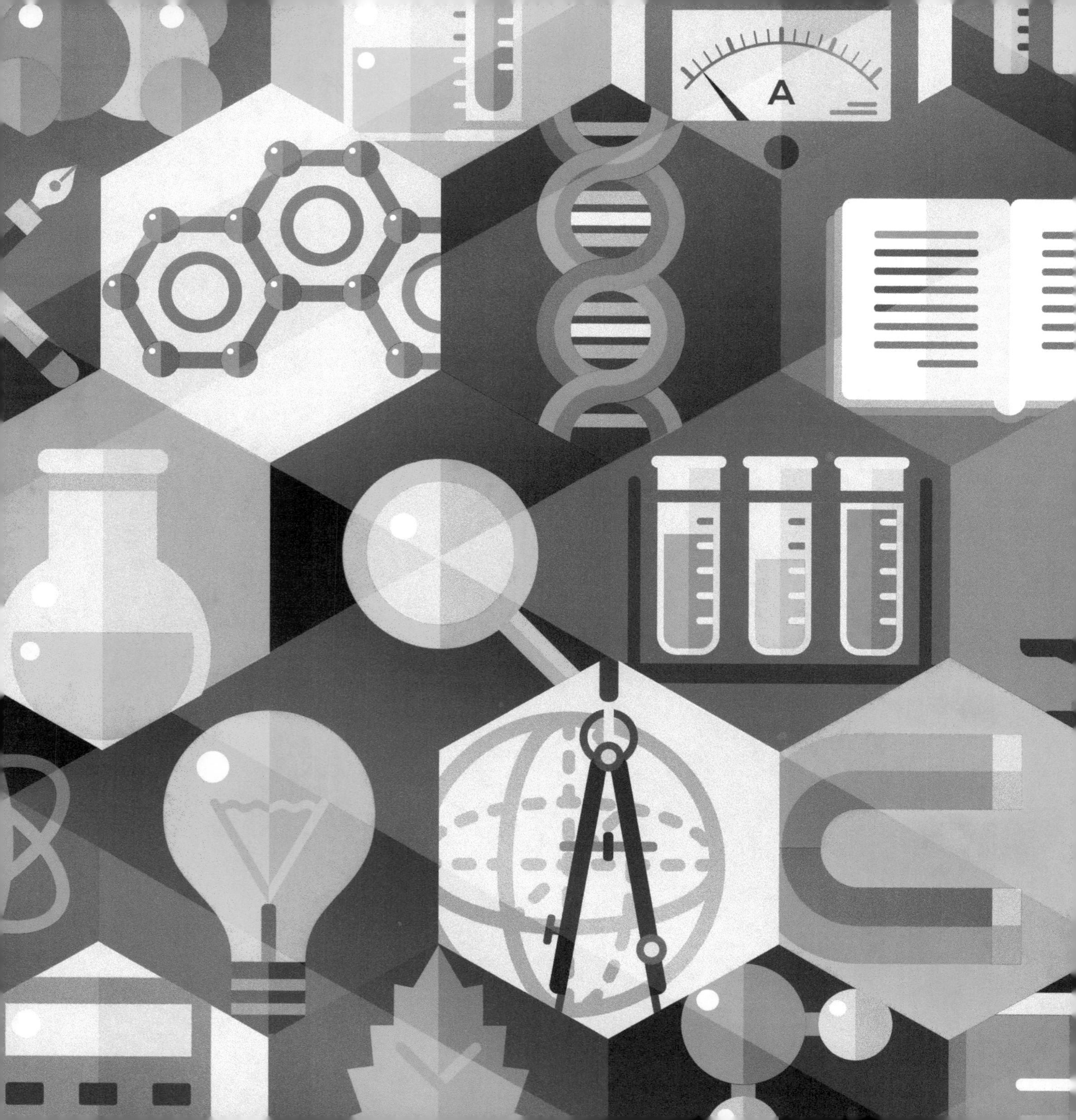
A

SUMMARY

In 1665, when Robert Hooke first looked at cork cells under a light microscope of his own design, he thought they looked like the rooms in a monastery called cellula. He coined the name "cells" for these new structures. Although his microscope was an improvement on other compound microscopes used previously, he didn't realize that he was looking at dead cells instead of living ones.

In 1838, over 170 years after Hooke's initial discoveries, colleagues Schwann and Schleiden began comparing the observations they were making about animal and plant cells, which led to the first conjectures about cell theory. Twenty years later, Rudolf Virchow firmed up these conjectures into the modern principles of cell theory that form the core of biology today. Thousands of experiments have supported the three basic tenets of modern cell theory.

Awesome! Now that you've learned about cell theory you may want to read about bacteria in the Baby Professor book, *Are All Bacteria Dangerous? Biology Book for Kids | Children's Biology Books.*

Visit
www.SpeedyBookStore.com
To view and download free content on your favorite subject and browse our catalog of new and exciting books for readers of all ages.

Printed in the USA
CPSIA information can be obtained
at www.ICGtesting.com
LVHW072002160124
769137LV00006B/48

9 781541 97456